ENCORE

More NFSPS Poetry Books Available Online

NFSPS CONTEST ANTHOLOGIES

Encore Prize Poems, Editor Kathy Lohrum Cotton
2016 • 2017 • 2018 • 2019

BlackBerryPeach Poetry Prizes, Editor Joseph Cavanaugh
2017 • 2018 • 2019

STEVENS POETRY MANUSCRIPT CONTEST WINNERS

Snake Breaking Medusa Disorder, Flower Conroy
Border Crossing, Amy Schmitz
A Landscape for Loss, Erin Rodoni
Midnight River, Laura Hansen
Beast, Mara Adamitz Scrupe
Breaking Weather, Betsy Hughes

COLLEGE UNDERGRADUATE POETRY CONTEST WINNERS

The Happening, Deanna Altomara
From the smoking courtyard, Caleb Rosenthal
A Monster the Size of the Sun, Iryna Klishch
Imperial Debris in Quisqueya and Beyond, Catherine Valdez
A Natural Cacophony, Sydney Lo
Exhales, Brian Selkirk
Elegy for Your Eyes, Anna Goodson
But Sometimes I Remember, Michael Welch
Here I Go, Torching, Carlina Duan
The Hole of Everything, Nebraska, Max Seifert

For other NFSPS titles
and previous editions visit
nfsps.com

ENCORE

Prize Poems
2019

Editor
Kathy Lohrum Cotton

National Federation of State Poetry Societies, Inc.
nfsps.com

Encore Prize Poems 2019

© 2019 as a collection by the National Federation of State Poetry Societies, Inc. (NFSPS), with first rights only. All rights to individual poems remain with the contributing poets. No part of this work may be reproduced or transmitted in any form or by any means, electronic or mechanical, or by use of any information storage or retrieval system, except as may be expressly permitted by the individual poet. We ask that credit be given to NFSPS when reprinting is granted. Individual authors confirm that these poems are their original creations, and to the publisher's knowledge these poems were written by the listed poets. NFSPS does not guarantee nor assume responsibility for verifying the authorship of each work.

Published July 2019
National Federation of State Poetry Societies, Inc.
nfsps.com

Edit and design by Kathy Lohrum Cotton
Transcription assistance by Diane Miller

Cover photo by Dino Reichmuth
NFSPS Medallion, David Nufer Photography
Title with permission of Alice Briley, Past President, NFSPS

ISBN-9781076228659

Printed in the United States of America

NATIONAL FEDERATION OF STATE POETRY SOCIETIES
Contests and Publications

NFSPS, organized in 1959, now umbrellas 31 state poetry societies and has nearly 4,000 members. The Federation is a non-profit organization, exclusively educational and literary and dedicated to the furtherance of poetry on the national level. It annually sponsors:

- **Fifty poetry contests** with cash prizes totaling more than $6,000, including a grand prize of $1,000, plus publication of each contest's top three winning poems in the annual *Encore* anthology.

- **The Stevens Poetry Manuscript Competition** for a single author's collection of poems, with a cash prize of $1,000 plus publication and 50 copies of the book.

- **The College Undergraduate Poetry (CUP) Competition** with two awards, the Meudt Memorial and Kahn Memorial, each offering $500 prizes, plus chapbook publication, 75 copies, and convention travel stipends.

- **The Manningham Trust Student Poetry Contest** which includes a junior division for grades 6–8 and senior division for grades 9–12. The top ten poems in each division at state-level competitions advance to the national contest. The top ten national winners in each division win cash prizes and publication in Manningham's annual anthology.

- **The BlackBerryPeach Prizes for Poetry: Spoken & Heard,** a performance poetry competition, awards three prizes—first place $1,000, second $500, and third $250, plus chapbook publication, performance video posting on YouTube, and convention travel stipends.

- **A national poetry convention,** hosted by a member state society, with poetry workshops, speakers, panel discussions, presentation of awards to contest winners, open-mic readings, and entertainment.

For further information, visit nfsps.com.

HONORARY CHANCELLORS

1960 Joseph Auslander	1974 Richard Armour	1995 Tess Gallagher
1962 John Crowe Ransom	1975 Richard Eberhart	1997 Michael Bugeja
1963 Glenn Ward Dresbach	1976 James Dickey	2000 David Wagoner
1964 Jesse Stuart	1977 Judson Jerome	2002 Maxine Kumin
1965 Grace Noll Crowell	1979 John Ciardi	2004 Naomi Shihab Nye
1966 Jean Starr Untermeyer	1981 Robert Coles	2006 Li Young Lee
1968 Loring Williams	1983 Richard Shelton	2008 Lewis Turco
1969 Harry M. Meachum	1985 Marcia Lee Masters	2010 Ted Kooser
1970 John Williams Andrews	1986 Robert Penn Warren	2012 Natasha Trethewey
1971 August Derleth	1987 Richard Wilber	2015 Peter Meinke
1972 William E. Stafford	1990 William E. Stafford	2018 Jo McDougall
1973 N. Scott Momaday	1992 Rodney Jones	2019 David Rothman

NFSPS PRESIDENTS

1959–1960	Cecilia Parsons Miller*	Pennsylvania Poetry Society
1960–1961	Clinton F. Larson*	Utah State Poetry Society
1961–1962	Robert D. West*	Ohio State Poetry Society
1962–1964	Edna Meudt*	Wisconsin Fellowship of Poets
1964–1966	Marvin Davis Winsett*	Poetry Society of Texas
1966–1968	Max C. Golightly*	Utah State Poetry Society
1968–1970	Hans Juergensen*	West Virginia Poetry Society
1970–1972	Russell Ferrall*	Wisconsin Fellowship of Poets
1972–1974	Jean Jenkins*	Utah State Poetry Society
1974–1976	Catherine Case Lubbe*	Poetry Society of Texas
1976–1978	Glenn Robert Swetman	Louisiana State Poetry Society
1978–1979	Carl P. Morton*	Alabama State Poetry Society
1979–1981	Alice Briley*	New Mexico State Poetry Society
1981–1983	Wauneta Hackleman*	Arizona State Poetry Society
1983–1885	Jack E. Murphy*	Poetry Society of Texas
1985–1987	Barbara Stevens*	South Dakota State Poetry Society
1987–1988	Henrietta A. Kroah*	Florida State Poets Association, Inc.
1988–1990	Jerry Robbins*	Kentucky State Poetry Society
1990–1992	Pat Stodghill	Poetry Society of Texas
1992–1994	Wanda B. Blaisdell*	Utah State Poetry Society
1994–1996	Ralph Hammond	Alabama State Poetry Society
1996–1998	Amy Jo Zook	Verse Writers Guild of Ohio
1998–2000	Susan Stevens Chambers	League of Minnesota Poets
2000–2002	Clarence P. Socwell	Utah State Poetry Society
2002–2004	Madelyn Eastlund	Florida State Poets Association, Inc.
2004–2006	Budd Powell Mahan	Poetry Society of Texas
2006–2008	Doris Stengel	League of Minnesota Poets
2008–2010	Nancy Baass	Poetry Society of Texas
2010–2012	Russell H. Strauss	Poetry Society of Tennessee
2012–2014	Jeremy Downes	Alabama State Poetry Society
2014–2016	Eleanor Berry	Oregon Poetry Association
2016–2018	Jim Barton*	Poets' Roundtable of Arkansas
2018–2020	Julie Cummings	Columbine Poets of Colorado

*Deceased

2019-2020 NFSPS EXECUTIVE AND APPOINTIVE BOARD MEMBERS

EXECUTIVE BOARD

President	Julie Cummings	CO
1st Vice President	Paul Ford	UT
2nd Vice President	Joseph Cavanaugh	FL
3rd Vice President	Charmaine Pappas Donovan	MN
4th Vice President	Steven Concert	PA
Chancellor	Polly Opsahl	MI
1st Vice Chancellor	Shirley Blackwell	NM
2nd Vice Chancellor	JoAn Howerton	TN
Secretary / Assistant Treasurer	Linda Harris	IA
Treasurer	Lucille Morgan Wilson	IA

APPOINTIVE BOARD

BlackBerryPeach Prizes for Poetry Chair	Joseph Cavanaugh	FL
Board Liaison to State Societies	Russell H. Strauss	TN
College Undergraduate Poetry Competition Chair	Steven Concert	PA
Contest Chair	Carla Jordan	CO
Contest Sponsors / Brochure Chair	Julie Cummings	CO
Convention Coordinator	Polly Opsahl	MI
Development Chair (Endowments/Sponsorships)	Joseph Cavanaugh	FL
Encore Editor	Kathy Lohrum Cotton	IL
Historian	Nancy Baass	TX
Judges Chair	JoAn Howerton	TN
Legal Counselor/Parliamentarian	Susan Stevens Chambers	MN
Librarian	Catherine L'Herisson	TX
Manningham Trust Competition Chair	Susan Stevens Chambers	MN
Manningham Trust Advisor	Sam Wood	NV
Membership Coordinator	Julie Cummings	CO
Poetry Day/Poetry Month Liaison Co-Chairs	Shirley Blackwell, NM......Amy Jo Zook	OH
Publicity Chair, Traditional Media	Amy Jo Zook	OH
Publicity Chair, Electronic Media	Julie Cummings, CO.........Lisa Salinas	TX
Special Awards	Charmaine Pappas Donovan	MN
Special Events / State Outreach Chair	Peter Stein	MN
Stevens Manuscript Competition Chair	Amanda Partridge	AR
Strophes Editor & Associate Editor	Paul Ford, UT .... Jim Lambert	IL
Webmaster	Billy Pennington	OK
Website Assistants	Julie Cummings, CO.............Paul Ford	UT
Youth Chair	Rosemerry Wahtola Trommer	CO

CONTENTS

NFSPS Contests and Publications v
NFSPS Chancellors and Presidents vi
NFSPS Board of Directors vii
Table of Contents with Contests, Sponsors, Judges, Contest Winners and Poem Titles viii
Foreword, Kathy Lohrum Cotton xv

1. NFSPS FOUNDERS AWARD (to honor Mary B. Wall), sponsored by NFSPS, Inc.
Judge Lynda La Rocca, Salida, CO
1st Wilda Morris, Bolingbrook, IL, "On the Local Train from Orvieto to Florence, Italy" 1
2nd Susan Stevens Chambers, Good Thunder, MN, "Planning a Poetry Party With a Cheese Head..." . 4
3rd Budd Powell Mahan, Dallas, TX, "When Spring Returns" 6

2. THE DIAMOND T AWARD, in memory of Harvey Jordan Turner sponsored by Diamond T Ranch Families
Judge Nicholas Trandahl, Upton, WY
1st Patricia Thrushart, Clarington, PA, "The Churchgoer" 7
2nd Sheila Moore, San Antonio, TX, "Canary Island Caballero" 8
3rd Crystie Cook, Sandy, UT, "Against Time" 9

3. THE NFSPS BOARD AWARD, sponsored by the NFSPS Executive and Appointive Boards
Judge Susan Glassmeyer, Cincinnati, OH
1st Paula J. Lambert, Dublin, OH, "Berkshire Mountains, September 2016" 11
2nd Jean Bell, Evergreen, CO, "Shadow Crossing" 12
3rd Dave Harvey, Talent, OR, "Dale Bassett, 1922–77" 13

4. THE MARGO AWARD, in memory of Margo LaGattuta, sponsored by Polly Opsahl
Judge Amy Irish, Lakewood, CO
1st Lynda La Rocca, Salida, CO, "Autumn Ritual" 14
2nd Doris Jones, Madison, MS, "Audience" 15
3rd Sarah Morin, Fishers, IN, "The Penguin" 16

5. WINNERS' CIRCLE AWARD, sponsored by Diane Glancy, Harriet Stovall Kelley, Pat Stodghill and Pat Underwood (previous prize winners in Contest 1, NFSPS Founders Award)
Judge Barbara Funke, Valparaiso, IN
1st Gwen Gunn, Guilford, CT, "Earthmother" 17
2nd David Bond, Carbondale, IL, "Reanimation" 18
3rd Patty Dickson Pieczka, Carbondale, IL, "Medieval Statue" 20

6. DONALD STODGHILL MEMORIAL AWARD, sponsored by Pat Stodghill
Judge Nancy Breen, Loveland, OH
1st Barbara Blanks, Garland, TX, "We're Not Going to Disneyland" 21
2nd Kathy Lohrum Cotton, Anna, IL, "A Few Slow Winter Bees" 22
3rd Christine Irving, Denton, TX, "Rendezvous on Ithaca" 23

7. GEORGIA POETRY SOCIETY AWARD, sponsored by the Georgia Poetry Society
Judge Carol Hamilton, Midwest City, OK
1st   Lorraine Jeffery, Orem, UT, "Saved" 24
2nd   Judith Tullis, Indian Head Park, IL, "Georgia Bite" 25
3rd   Geraldine Felt, Layton, UT, "Saint Simons Island, Georgia" 26

8. POETRY SOCIETY OF TEXAS AWARD, sponsored by the Poetry Society of Texas
Judge Karen Bailey, Blanchard, OK
1st   Terry Miller, Richmond, TX, "A Whisper in Dime Box" 28
2nd   Kathy Lohrum Cotton, Anna, IL, "Old Poet at the Open Mic" 29
3rd   Beth Staas, Oak Brook, IL, "Family Album" 30

9. THE CHILDREN'S HOUR AWARD, sponsored by the Turner and Rabke families in honor of grandchildren everywhere
Judge Shelly Reed Thieman, Des Moines, IA
1st   Harvey Stone, Johnson City, TN, "The Drop" 31
2nd   Kolette Montague, Centerville, UT, "Flower Power" 32
3rd   Jerri Hardesty, Brierfield, AL, "Wild Party" 33

10. AL LASTER MEMORIAL AWARD, ekphrastic poetry, sponsored by Diana Gagne
Judge Sharon Mishler Fox, Knoxville, TN
1st   Amy Irish, Lakewood, CO, "The Winged Nike (of Nevada)" 34
2nd   Linda Eve Diamond, Port Orange, FL, "Surreally Good Apple" 36
3rd   Robin Gow, Mineola, NY, "flowers 1964" 38

11. FLORIDA STATE POETS ASSOCIATION, INC. AWARD, sponsored by the Florida State Poets Assn., Inc.
Judge Donna Salli, West Brainerd, MN
1st   Micki Blenkush, St. Cloud, MN, "Riding the Down and Up Waves" 39
2nd   Janet Watson, Wesley Chapel, FL, "The Highest Range" 40
3rd   Doris Jones, Madison, MS, "Beachside Jazz" 41

12. ALABAMA STATE POETRY SOCIETY AWARD, sponsored by the Alabama State Poetry Society
Judge Bruce Eastman, West Brainerd, MN
1st   Gwen Gunn, Guilford, CT, "Found Gift" 42
2nd   Patricia Barnes, Wyandotte, MI, "Napping Baby" 43
3rd   John W. Coppock, Tuttle, OK, "Reflection" 44

13. LAND OF ENCHANTMENT AWARD, sponsored by the New Mexico State Poetry Society
Judge Deanna Baldelli, Elizabeth, CO
1st   Christian Shute, Cheyenne, WY, "King of the Cul de Sac" 45
2nd   Nancy Breen, Loveland, OK, "Virginia Specter" 46
3rd   Maxine Carlson, Iowa City, IA, "Note to His New Wife" 47

14. THE VIRGINA CORRIE-COZART MEMORIAL AWARD, sponsored by friends in the Peregrine Writers
Judge Carol Willette Bachofner, Rockland, ME
1st   Claudia Van Gerven, Boulder, CO, "When the Trees Escaped" 48

2nd Lorrie Wolfe, Windsor, CO, "Marks on Paper" 49
3rd Marleine Yanish, Denver, CO, "Becoming Music" 50

15. ARIZONA STATE POETRY SOCIETY AWARD, sponsored by the Arizona State Poetry Society
Judge Nancy Cook, St. Paul, MN
1st Robert E. Blenheim, Daytona Beach, FL, "A Wet Dream in a Dry Season" 51
2nd Julie Shavin, Fountain, CO, "Judging the Cover" 52
3rd Meredith R. Cook, Blue Earth, MN, "Never Land Sixty-Six Years Later:" 53

16. MILDRED VORPAHL BAASS REMEMBRANCE AWARD, sponsored by her daughter, Nancy Baass
Judge Julia George, Muskegon, MI
1st Cynthia Nankee, Canton, MI, "(Not Quite) Still Life in the Garden: Black Cat with Pumpkins" ... 54
2nd Robert Schinzel, Highland Village, TX, "If Winter Comes…" 55
3rd Carol Williams, York, PA, "Long-Haired Cat" 56

17. LEAGUE OF MINNESOTA POETS AWARD, in memory or John Rezmerski, sponsored by the League of Minnesota Poets
Judge Cathy Essinger, Troy, OH
1st Rita Geil, Carson City, NV, "Directions for Daughters" 57
2nd Diane Glancy, Gainesville, TX, "A Night on the Lake" 58
3rd Barbara Blanks, Garland, TX, "Out for Blood" 59

18. JESSICA C. SAUNDERS MEMORIAL AWARD, sponsored by the Shavano Poets Society of Colorado
Judge Cathy Moran, Little Rock, AR
1st Charmaine Pappas Donovan, Brainerd, MN, "Storm Phobia" 60
2nd Wendy Visser, Cambridge, Ontario, "Adrift" 61
3rd Jana Bouma, Madison Lake, MN, "Postponement" 62

19. POETRY SOCIETY OF INDIANA AWARD, sponsored by the Poetry Society of Indiana
Judge Pat Durmon, Norfork, AR
1st Beth Staas, Oak Brook, IL, "Worship" 63
2nd Diane Glancy, Gainesville, TX, "Yellowtail Lanes, Lodge Grass, Montana" 64
3rd Laurie Kolp, Beaumont, TX, "Community Comes Out in Troubled Times" 65

20. NEVADA POETRY SOCIETY AWARD, sponsored by the Nevada Poetry Society
Judge Susan Gundlach, Evanston, IL
1st Tony Fusco, West Haven, CT, "The Flag Is Upside Down" 66
2nd Paula J. Lambert, Dublin, OH, "Siege" 67
3rd Gail Denham, Sunriver, OR, "Items I Read Last Year" 68

21. WILLIAM STAFFORD MEMORIAL AWARD, sponsored by the Oregon Poetry Association and friends
Judge Rita Moritz, Pell City, AL
1st LaVern Spencer McCarthy, Blair, OK, "The Old, Yellow School Bus" 69
2nd Caroline Johnson, Willow Springs, IL, "Cancer" 70
3rd Catherine Moran, Little Rock, AR, "All the forgotten pieces" 71

22. THE NEW YORK POETRY FORUM AWARD, sponsored by the New York Poetry Forum
Judge Jo McDougall, Little Rock, AR
1st   Andrea McBride, Wesley Chapel, FL, "Writing Outside" 72
2nd   Martha H. Balph, Millville, UT, "Flight" 73
3rd   Robert Schinzel, Highland Village, TX, "Whiteout" 74

23. COLUMBINE POETS OF COLORADO AWARD, sponsored by the Columbine Poets of Colorado
Judge Jerri Hardesty, Brierfield, AL
1st   Jean Bell, Evergreen, CO, "Sarcasm in December" 75
2nd   James B. Mele, Bristol, CT, "August" 76
3rd   Diane Glancy, Gainesville, TX, "March" 77

24. MORTON D. PROUTY & ELSIE S. PROUTY MEMORIAL AWARD, sponsored by daughters Catherine Prouty Horn and Carol Prouty Ostberg and their families
Judge Art Elser, Denver, CO
1st   Stephen Curry, Jackson, MS, "Nature's Law" 78
2nd   Kathy Lohrum Cotton, Anna, IL, "Amargosa, the Hide-and-Seek River" 79
3rd   Sarah Morin, Fishers, IN, "Stalactite/Stalagmite" 80

25. POETS' ROUNDTABLE OF ARKANSAS AWARD, sponsored by Catherine Moran
Judge Sandra Nantais, Arcadia, LA
1st   Karen Kay Bailey, Blanchard, OK, "The Neglected Gift" 81
2nd   Mark Barton, Mechanicsburg, PA, "Sighting Birdsong in the Pyrenées" 82
3rd   Barbara Blanks, Garland, TX, "Yesterday" 83

26. LOUISIANA STATE POETRY SOCIETY AWARD, sponsored by Louisiana State Poetry Society
Judge Sue Brannan Walker, East Mobile, AL
1st   John W. Coppock, Tuttle, OK, "from SYMPOSIUM—A Play: No. 1 and No. 2" 84
2nd   J. Paul Holcomb, Double Oak, TX, "I Never Liked That Tie Anyway" 85
3rd   Christine H. Boldt, Temple, TX, "The Place for Lost Children" 86

27. FREEDA MURPHY MEMORIAL AWARD, sponsored by the Poetry Society of Texas
Judge Doug Rutledge, Columbus, OH
1st   Catherine Moran, Little Rock, AR, "Crisis hot-line" 87
2nd   Fay Guinn, Jonesboro, AR, "Too Much Bliss" 88
3rd   Diane Glancy, Gainesville, TX, "Card Stock" 89

28. CLAIRE VAN BREEMAN DOWNES MEMORIAL AWARD, sponsored by Alan Downes
Judge Stacy Pendergrast, Little Rock, AR
1st   Mary Tindall, Whitehouse, TX, "Doll" 90
2nd   Catherine Moran, Little Rock, AR, "Discovering pigs" 91
3rd   Janet Watson, Wesley Chapel, FL, "At a Fundraiser for Cancer Victims" 92

29. UTAH STATE POETRY SOCIETY AWARD, sponsored by the Utah State Poetry Society
Judge Julie Cummings, Conifer, CO
1st   Wendy Visser, Cambridge, Ontario, "Remnants" 93

2nd Lucille Morgan Wilson, Des Moines, IA, "Tracks Through Winter" 94
3rd Laura Altshul, New Haven, CT, "Family of Six Portrait, 1918" 95

30. CSPS JAMES E. MacWHINNEY MEMORIAL AWARD, sponsored by the California State Poetry Society
Judge Jeanette Willert, Pell City, AL
1st Barbara J. Funke, St. George, UT, "The Invention of Nouns" 96
2nd Alison Chisholm, Birkdale, U.K., "Double Exposure" 97
3rd Loretta Diane Walker, Odessa, TX, "Aftermath" 98

31. ILLINOIS STATE POETRY SOCIETY AWARD, sponsored by the Illinois State Poetry Society
Judge Sandra Soli, Edmond, OK
1st Caroline Johnson, Willow Springs, IL, "On Listening to Middle Eastern Poetry..." 99
2nd Kathy Lohrum Cotton, Anna, IL, "Two Views of the Plaza" 100
3rd Crystie Cook, Sandy, UT, "Booksmarts" 101

32. OHIO AWARD, sponsored by the Ohio Poetry Association
Judge Jessica Temple, Huntsville, AL
1st Joshua Conklin, Amherst, NH, "Ode to the Cochlea" 102
2nd Kathy Lohrum Cotton, Anna, IL, "Lightning Rod" 103
3rd Markay Brown, St. George, UT, "Undressing Billy Collins" 104

33. MINUTE AWARD, sponsored by Sharon Martin Turner
Judge Rose Klix, Johnson City, TN
1st Richard Hurzeler, Tyler, TX, "Where Worlds Collide" 105
2nd Jerri Hardesty, Brierfield, AL, "Random Act" 106
3rd V. Kimball Barney, Kaysville, UT, "Wishful Fishing" 107

34. POETRY SOCIETY OF MICHIGAN AWARD, sponsored by the Poetry Society of Michigan
Judge Janice Hornburg, Johnson City, TN
1st Micki Blenkush, St. Cloud, MN, "This Year's Garden" 108
2nd Dave Harvey, Talent, OR, "A Sign, a Jingle" 109
3rd Robert Schinzel, Highland Village, TX, "A Long View Through Time" 110

35. MISSISSIPPI POETRY SOCIETY AWARD, sponsored by the Mississippi Poetry Society, Inc.
Judge Carolyn Files, Oak Ridge, LA
1st Budd Powell Mahan, Dallas, TX, "The Vietnam Memorial" 111
2nd Dave Harvey, Talent, OR, "Deadly Birds" 112
3rd Lisa Toth Salinas, Spring, TX, "To the Former Child: Directions for Your Day" 113

36. JESSE STUART MEMORIAL AWARD, sponsored by the Kentucky State Poetry Society
Judge Chris McCurry, Lexington, KY
1st Maurine Haltiner, Salt Lake City, UT, "Nosing About the Stars" 114
2nd Susan Maxwell Campbell, Mansfield, TX, "Graft: Kisses and Roses" 115
3rd Judith Feenstra, Maple Lake, MN, "Stray Cat Traveling" 116

37. HUMOROUS POETRY AWARD, sponsored by Ziggies Presents!
Judge Ann Carolyn Cates, Southaven, MS
1st   Curt Vevang, Palatine, IL, "The Grandpa Card" 117
2nd   Sarah Morin, Fishers, IN, "Checklist for the Picnic" 118
3rd   Lorraine Jeffery, Orem, UT, "New Bird Feeder" 119

38. BARBARA STEVENS MEMORIAL AWARD, sponsored by Susan Stevens Chambers, Christina Flaugher, and Colin Chambers.
Judge Christina Flaugher, Mapleton, MN
1st   Budd Powell Mahan, Dallas, TX, "Smoke" 120
2nd   Trina Lee, Oklahoma City, OK, "Somewhere" 121
3rd   Larry Schulte, Albuquerque, NM, "Home" 122

39. ALICE MACKENZIE SWAIM MEMORIAL AWARD, sponsored by Pennsylvania Poetry Society, Inc.
Judge Florence Bruce, Memphis, TN
1st   Budd Powell Mahan, Dallas, TX, "Blood on the Mountain" 123
2nd   Joyce Shiver, Crystal River, FL, "Cicada Summer" 124
3rd   J. Paul Holcomb, Double Oak, TX, "Changing Seasons, Changing Colors" 125

40. POETRY SOCIETY OF OKLAHOMA AWARD, in memory of Clark Elliott sponsored by the Poetry Society of Oklahoma
Judge Janet Qually, Memphis, TN
1st   Barbara Blanks, Garland, TX, "Like His Ancestors" 126
2nd   Joshua Conklin, Amherst, NH, "Questioning" 127
3rd   Dena R. Gorrell, Edmond, OK, "Sometimes All That Glitters Isn't Gold" 128

41. SAVE OUR EARTH AWARD, sponsored by Martha H. Balph in memory of David F. Balph
Judge Alan Perry, Maple Grove, MN
1st   Christina M. Flaugher, Mapleton, MN, "Letter to the Daughter I Didn't Have" 129
2nd   Amy Irish, Lakewood, CO, "The Children of the Earth" 130
3rd   Micki Blenkush, St. Cloud, MN, "From the Voice of Water" 131

42. MASSACHUSETTS STATE POETRY SOCIETY AWARD, sponsored by Massachusetts State Poetry Society
Judge Russell Strauss, Memphis, TN
1st   Beth Staas, Oak Brook, IL, "Spring Demon" 132
2nd   Christine H. Boldt, Temple, TX, "Middle School Choir Concert" 133
3rd   Pat Underwood, Colfax, IA, "Colostomy" 134

43. POETRY SOCIETY OF TENNESSEE AWARD, sponsored by the Poetry Society of Tennessee
Judge Jennifer Horne, Cottondale, AL
1st   Alison Chisholm, Birkdale, U.K., "One Moment in Time" 135
2nd   Brenda Brown Finnegan, Ocean Springs, MS, "A Different Thanksgiving" 136
3rd   LaVern Spencer McCarthy, Blair, OK, "He Loves Me Still..." 137

44. IOWA POETRY ASSOCIATION AWARD, sponsored by the Iowa Poetry Association
Judge Susan Cherry, Evanston, IL
1st   Martha H. Balph, Millville, UT, "Spinach".. 138
2nd   Linda R. Payne, Cincinnati, OH, "Summer Rain".. 139
3rd   Marjorie Dohlman, Riceville, IA, "A to Zoo" 140

45. WYOPOETS AWARD, sponsored by the Wyopoets of Wyoming
Judge Ann Gasser, West Reading, PA
1st   Susan Daubenspeck, Corpus Christi, TX, "Singing Red Sky"................................... 141
2nd   Cheryl A. Van Beek, Wesley Chapel, FL, "Enchanted" 142
3rd   O. William Asplund, Layton, UT, "Roundup Memories" 143

46. SAN ANTONIO POETS ASSOCIATION AWARD, sponsored by the San Antonio Poets Association, a chapter of the Poetry Society of Texas
Judge William Reyer, Tiffin, OH
1st   Budd Powell Mahan, Dallas, TX, "The Grandfather Clock" 144
2nd   Lorraine Jeffery, Orem, UT, "Canning" 145
3rd   Robert Schinzel, Highland Village, TX, "Kachinas on First Mesa"........................... 146

47. MAINE POETS SOCIETY AWARD, sponsored by the Maine Poets Society
Judge Bruce Bond, Denton, TX
1st   Crystie Cook, Sandy UT, "Observation at Oceanside Beach, California".................. 147
2nd   Christine H. Boldt, Temple, TX, "The Compass Rose" 148
3rd   Julie Shavin, Fountain, CO, "Hope's Cloak"... 149

48. MIRIAM S. STRAUSS MEMORIAL AWARD, sponsored by Russell H. Strauss
Judge Julie Allyn Johnson, Norwalk, IA
1st   Laura Trigg, Little Rock, AR, "This Is the City That Birthed Me"............................. 150
2nd   Susan Maxwell Campbell, Mansfield, TX, "From Up Here " 151
3rd   Omair Hasan, Toledo, OH, "Poetry open mic at a busy café but I do not speak"....... 153

49. THE POETS NORTHWEST AWARD, sponsored by Poets Northwest, a Poetry Society of Texas chapter
Judge Vivian Stewart, Oklahoma City, OK
1st   Gail Denham, Sunriver, OR, "Evenings Among The Junipers" 154
2nd   Beth Staas, Oak Brook, IL, "The Challenge".. 155
3rd   Barbara Blanks, Garland, TX, "Isolation" 156

50. STUDENT AWARD, Grades 9 through 12, sponsored by Nancy Baass and Catherine L'Herisson
Judge Tamara Baxter, Kingsport, TN
1st   Laura Liu, Wayne, PA, "aurelia".. 157
2nd   Krystal Smith, Little Rock, AR, "Don't Shoot" 158
3rd   Mary Margaret Sell, Dallas, TX, "Mackey Walks Me" 159

Index by Author with Poem Title 160
Honorable Mentions by Author with Contest and Award... 164
2019 Contests... 169

FOREWORD
Encore, Prize Poems 2019

In this 2019 edition of *Encore*, the National Federation of State Poetry Societies presents the top 150 prize-winning poems read and awarded at the national convention in Santa Fe, New Mexico. Selected from nearly 7,000 submissions, these winning poems present the diverse responses of poets from states across the U.S., as well as the United Kingdom and Canada.

The 50 contests challenged authors to write in the structured forms of pantoum, villanelle, 13-line trimeric, traditional sonnet, 60-syllable minute, and iambic pentameter blank verse. They provoked fresh, personal interpretations of themes as wide-ranging as cowboy poetry and cats, ekphrastic poems and environmental issues, the seacoast and Wyoming. Each contest's subject or form and the contest name are listed above the poems so you can share in the poets' inspirations as well as constraints.

Illinois poet Wilda Morris opens the 2019 *Encore* with her $1,000 prize-winning poem, "On the Local Train from Orvieto to Florence, Italy"; students from Pennsylvania, Arkansas and Texas close it with impressive selections by our youngest poets, grades 9–12. Between those pages lie sorrow and humor, wisdom and passion, and the uniqueness of many voices on many subjects. We invite you to explore cover-to-cover.

We also welcome you to learn more about the National Federation of State Poetry Societies and our member state societies. Note the lists of our contests, publications and leadership. For more information, visit nfsps.com.

Kathy Lohrum Cotton, Editor
Encore, Prize Poems 2019

NFSPS FOUNDERS AWARD, Contest 1 (Any Subject)
First Place, Wilda Morris, Bolingbrook, IL

On the Local Train from Orvieto to Florence, Italy
for Ed

Orvieto
I came to the hill town without you.
I saw your face in the frescoes
of ancient churches, your footprints
on cobblestones. I wanted to buy you
a gelato and take you to the cathedral
to hear the viola da gamba, lute, drum
and double recorder. The tears–
of yesterday's rain, dry on the train
window, obscure my view as we pull
out of the station. Longing is my only companion.

Fabro-Ficulle
When the train emerges from tunnels, I see
the haze has lifted from hills and valley.
Outside town, field hands have finished
the harvest, returned to lovers
who offered them focaccia, cheese and wine.
My hands are empty.

Chianciano Terme
On the train platform, a man
with a red suitcase stands, like you do,
with hands in jeans pockets,
but they are not your pockets.
They are not your hands.

Castiglione del Lago
Sprigs of green cover fields like winter wheat
planted where you took me to meet your Kansas kin.
I keep looking for the lake. I think it has learned
your game of absence. Finally, past the station, I see
the blue water, but no brown eyes.

Terontola
For what does the train wait so long?
Are you waiting for me?

Camucia-Cortona
A couple, old as us, has come down from this,
another hill town that gleams in November sun.
They board the train together.

Castiglion Fiorentino
We pass vineyards already harvested
and vineyards still heavy with fruit.
Left longer, the wine merchant said,
grapes make sweeter wine. Does your love
grow sweeter as I tarry here?

Arezzo
Persimmon boughs hang heavy
with the fruit of love.

Ponticino and *Bucine*
We do not stop. These are trips we did not take,
the children we did not birth, everything
we avoided, forgot, neglected, left undone.
Everything fate keeps from us.

Montevarchi
A woman has hung a blanket to dry,
airs pillows on the ledge of an open window.
When will we lay our heads together?

San Giovanni Valdarno
Church bells, silent as we pass.
In the station, a couple shares
a long hug. Welcome home?
Goodbye?

Figline
The conductor announces connections
to Bologna, where you took me
when we were young.

Firenze Campo di Marte
The conductor has come to check tickets.
I neglected to put mine in the green box
on the station platform in Orvieto.
He could fine me but just gives me a warning.

Firenze Santa Maria Novella
I will seek you on these ancient streets.
I will gaze at Michelangelo's David,
but your hand will not be the one
holding the slingshot. I will find
Donatello's David, but the boots
he wears are not your boots,
his hat is not your hat.
In my room, I will be alone,
my bed cold, as I listen for your whisper.

Planning a Poetry Party with a Cheese Head of Billy Collins

Mavis Engstrom has carved it, using
excellent sharp-Wisconsin-cheddar.
She's done a pretty good job.
It looks just like the picture on
the back of his fourth book.
We all said this was great—
a way to have Billy come to our party
since there is no way we can afford his
twenty-thousand-dollar-fee-plus-additional-costs
if we wanted him to lead a panel discussion
as well as give the keynote address.

So, this is even better—since we get to nibble on him.
Especially if you don't look at his one ear,
which is off somewhat symmetrically—and a little big
in proportion to the rest of his head.
But we'll stick the knife right into that ear
so no-one will notice. For that matter
his whole head is bigger than life-sized,
but whose wouldn't be at twenty thousand a pop?

I'm sure Dorothy will want to snap some pictures
before we cut into him—she has done her workshop
four times on his "Shoveling Snow with Buddha"
although we never really knew for certain
if she got the true message of the poem.

Everyone is pretty sure Jason Winslow
doesn't even know who Billy is.
He is bound to dip exactly into B.C.'s eyes
because of the way the cheese whips up there.
He won't worry about disturbing the big man.
Don't you like the way the Triscuit wheat
crackers tuck around his chin?

NFSPS FOUNDERS AWARD, CONTEST 1 (ANY SUBJECT)

In any event, the party really isn't about B.C.,
it's an excuse to gather all our local poets together,
drink a little wine:
although Henry and Dennis will probably
switch to Miller Beer halfway through the night.
We will read some of our favorite poems,
meaning our own, of course.

We will eat a *lot* of cheese—
so by ten or ten thirty
all that will be left
on the empty red platter of Billy's head
will be some good Wisconsin cheddar crumbs
which I am thinking about gathering up
into a good Hollandaise sauce
for Eggs Benedict tomorrow.

I think I can shape them into
a pretty good likeness of Sharon Olds.

NFSPS FOUNDERS AWARD, Contest 1 (Any Subject)
Third Place, Budd Powell Mahan, Dallas, TX

When Spring Returns
A Gloss

I have a rendezvous with Death
At some disputed barricade.
When Spring comes back with rustling shade
And apple-blossoms fill the air.
~Alan Seeger, "I Have a Rendezvous with Death"

I have a rendezvous with death
as every man must come to learn.
I know my fate, but do not burn
for detail of the face unmet.
I cannot fear nor dare forget
I have a rendezvous with death.

At some disputed barricade
the spirit will give up its fight
as youth's bravado basks in light
of consummate transcendent days.
Each life will cede defiant ways
at some disputed barricade.

When spring comes back with rustling shade
I cherish petal, blade, and leaf,
refuse the thought of mortal grief,
immerse in attar, sun, and breeze.
I sonnet birds, and haiku bees
when spring comes back with rustling shade.

And apple blossoms fill the air,
when April cloaks mortality
with bursting bloom and greening tree.
December's icy presence dims
as breezes lift up stiffened limbs,
and apple blossoms fill the air.

THE DIAMOND T AWARD, Contest 2 (Cowboy Poetry)

First Place, Patricia Thrushart, Clarington, PA

The Churchgoer

He was of an indeterminate age
with his bowed head, gray angel-wing
temples, and a sag in his shoulders
that made more sense on a barstool
than a church pew, where he sat
half-mumbling Amazing Grace
and looking like he felt anything but amazing;
as if his heart
was beating a different rhythm,
the one on a jukebox playing slow country songs
about lessons that only life outside
four holy walls could teach.

I threw in a five and passed the collection plate to him,
and made contact with his lidded red eyes,
because I have a soft spot
for the wild sad cowboy inside each of us.

Later, at the sign,
his handshake told me something
I already knew.

THE DIAMOND T AWARD, CONTEST 2 (COWBOY POETRY)
Second Place, Sheila Moore, San Antonio, TX

Canary Island Caballero*

White Stetson held high in right hand, left hand steady
on the reigns of a golden palomino rearing on command,
a twenty-year-old caballero, direct Canary Island
descendant, smiles from a seventy-year-old sepia photo.

But I knew him as Uncle Bill, a hard working, joke telling
man whose presence filled a room and who worked
from *can* to *can't*, he liked to say, herding hundreds
of Brahmans, riding fence lines, branding calves, breaking
green horses—never-ending chores of pulling himself up by
his bootstraps, carving an empire from nothing for family.

At the sound of welcome dinner bell, he and his brothers
trudged in from hot range for lunch. A halo circled
black hair where sweat-stained Stetson had sat,
face and hands cleaned outside in the "wash-room," dusty
boots waiting outside on the back porch. Grace said, they
made short shrift of mounds of buttered mashed potatoes,
rice and steak, vegetables from the garden, and fresh,
berry cobbler washed down with strong black coffee.

After "dinner" (clothes too grimy for good furniture)
they'd lie prone like scattered fence posts
on the shade-cooled veranda, snoring a quick siesta
before more coffee and back to bone-breaking work.

I recalled the sight of those hard-working men
when I visited Uncle Bill that last time. He lay still
as an abandoned saddle, whittled down by age
and too weak to offer anything but a feeble smile
before taking his last siesta.

*Descendant of first Spanish settlers in San Antonio.

Against Time

*Inspired by my grandfather, Ray Cook, 1914–2005,
who had sheep and cows in Utah and Wyoming*

The November wind, fitful and urgent,
sounds a wolf-like knell
as it rips through the air in hurried descent
and rushes down the ridge of pinyon pine.
It cuts through densely-growing sagebrush,
moans and whistles in a high-pitched whine,
then turns to batter the old, wooden bridge
which crosses the now-dry ravine.

It's the end of Indian summer,
and time is blowing away in the wind,
with winter's first storm determined to arrive full blast.

Whitened clay, parched and cracked,
curls up at the edges like stale tortilla shells.
A cowboy on horseback rides along the swell
of these foothills, covered by still-green
juniper trees, all their trunks and limbs
defined by fibrous eddies,
gnarled and knobbed, doubling back
like whorls of a fingerprint,
their curves as elegant and rough
as Van Gogh's vigorous paintbrush strokes.
The wind swallows the sound
and sight of three stray cows.
The cowboy halts his horse, a gray Appaloosa,
hindquarters speckled white
as the ravine's dry clay. He dismounts
to more closely examine cowtail hair
snagged on a low tree branch,
squints against the whirling dirt.

His eyes narrow to peer through the juniper
in search of the three stray cows.

Tension constricts his throat—
time is short before the storm hits.
His livestock wanders alone in these hills,
with only a strand of time left in which to be found.

Berkshire Mountains, September 2016

Who can open the door who does not reach for the latch? ~Mary Oliver

Oh, friend. Do you know I follow you these ghost-lit mornings, picking up
the Marlboro butts and Red Bull cans you leave behind at night? My father

picked up Lucky Strikes and Pabst Blue Ribbon—the trash your father left.
When he sometimes found an unopened can, he brought it home to mother

who made beer bread, warm and lovely, to set beside our dinner. Had you any
way of knowing what you left behind could nourish? And it's true, my friend:

we judged you. We'd see the remnants of your party fires and wonder why,
coming here, you refuse the silence this place offers. Had we thought more

kindly, we might have seen you crave it, too, this silence, and fear it—
like we do. We all carry the same memories. The same ghosts haunt us all.

Monsters can't be wrestled to the ground, and God knows they won't be
ignored. They leave when we look them in the eye, full daylight, unfettered

by smoke or haze; they leave when we let them go. It's why I walk this trail,
to watch the ghosts of my dad and your dad and you all disappear, to watch

the ghosts of even me begin to fade. I find a place for us all to sit in silence,
watching this world so alive: oak and acorn, duck and doe and damselfly.

You know we are most a part of the world when the world does not take notice?
It's been my hardest lesson. I feared you'd never know me, friend, that I might

live and die alone. Is it your fear, too? Is it why you leave so much behind?
Oh, friend. The air I take in this morning is the same you exhaled last night,

the same these damsels floated on when both our dads were here. We are,
together, that lovely bread my mother baked from the gift of your dad's beer.

Shadow Crossing

Suffering took the first step, our journey
fueled by fear, feet persecuted into flight
by the violence of hopeless tomorrows.

Along the way we ate moonlight and shadows
slept the waking hours on dreamless deserts
drank tears from wellsprings of the heart.

Along the way coyotes howled a lonely warning
the child who stumbled a new burden for the trail
desperate when there was no turning back.

By grace delivered at what we believed
our destination, arrival its own reward for endurance
our feet hungry to plant in new soil

only to discover we continue as strangers
in the promised land, detention and denial
yet stand between us and safe refuge.

Now we dwell in an eerie forest of twilights
not knowing if half-gray is dawn of hope
or prelude to deep night of dejection.

In shadow we remain, essentially the same
propelled by necessity, burdened by borders, still
searching for a future willing to welcome us home.

THE NFSPS BOARD AWARD, Contest 3 (Walk a Mile)
Third Place, Dave Harvey, Talent, OR

Dale Bassett, 1922–77
A Spoon River Poem

I died in the dead lands, the Funeral Mountains.
When they said this cancer would take me in months,
and tried to get me into a hospital,
I said, the hell with that!
Took me a week to walk to Death Valley.
I camped a night at Stovepipe Wells,
then walked on east, into these stony peaks.
I was alone, pains growing.
It was tough, but never as tough as Italy or Korea,
and nowhere near as tough as losing Flo.

At least there were no plastic tubes and hospital beds,
the floors gleaming or puke-spotted,
and the sky and I shut away from each other.
Now my meat's bound up in other bodies:
that coyote, trotting across these high basins,
owls and night hawks, coming in by moonlight,
and those buzzards, circling above the highest peaks.
My bones? They may be here forever.

My whole life came down to this:
two wars, work, marriage to Flo,
hiking wild-country trails with her
and later with friends who all seemed to pass—too soon.
At last, nothing—and nobody—left to lose.

It was freedom to come here and die.

I chose it.
I tasted it.
It was bitter.
It was good.

THE MARGO AWARD, CONTEST 4 (ANIMALS)

First Place, Lynda La Rocca, Salida, CO

Autumn Ritual

In my dream,
bones click and clatter,
wind-chime ghosts are signaling the end
of all that once was sweet
and slow and summer warm.

Outside my window,
open still
to catch the final cricket's rasp,
two bucks are battling.
I wake,
I rise,
their antlers silhouetted, stark,
their circles raising midnight dust
that could corona all the moon
and halo all the vast and brooding,
bruised-black sky.

One buck is thick and heavy,
one is smaller, just as sure,
and neither will give way, give ground,
and now the two are whirling,
locked together in some ancient dance
that I can see and hear and smell—
the rhythmic huffs and snorts and grunts,
the grass is crushed and dying.
They're putting on a show
but not for me.
The antlers clash,
and I am nothing to them,
I am nothing.
I cannot stop the days from dropping
down into the darkness,
and I cannot,
am not asked to,
join the dance.

THE MARGO AWARD, CONTEST 4 (ANIMALS)

Second Place, Doris Jones, Madison, MS

Audience

Rose-tone clouds eavesdrop
at day's edge, seizing whispered secrets,
then passing choice tidbits
to a thousand attentive sparrows.

THE MARGO AWARD, CONTEST 4 (ANIMALS)

Third Place, Sarah Morin, Fishers, IN

The Penguin

Penguin, bird of contradiction,
your lack of flight is no affliction.
You get on with life swimmingly:
half on land and half on sea.

Your costume, too, is quite abnormal:
naked, yet dressed up so formal
for cold life of no luxury:
half on land and half on sea.

How can you attract a mate
with your shuffling, awkward gait?
Yet penguins bond romantically
half on land and half on sea.

As parents, you never think twice
to waddle miles across the ice
from feeding grounds to nursery:
half on land and half on sea.

You teach your fuzzy sons and daughters
to fly with flippers through the water.
Bumbling birds move elegantly
half on land and half on sea.

You don't fit in with your bird cousins.
Let them take flight in their dozens!
Your world's a perfect binary,
half on land and half on sea.

First Place, Gwen Gunn, Guilford, CT

Earthmother

I drove along
route four and flew into
a thousand pieces hanging in the
round gray sky and looking down on
who was once a fairly single woman when
her child implored the pieces *see the airplane*
so persistently that they remembered how
her birth had proffered strength to
coalesce so Molly bloomed
and I said *yes*

WINNERS' CIRCLE, CONTEST 5 (ANY SUBJECT)

Second Place, David Bond, Carbondale, IL

Reanimation
for Gabriel

It's hard to ignore
your adeptness at

quickening the dead
with chemicals and

eyes of glass, now
that you've staggered

wild with love and whiskey
across the charred

garden to a Browning
cradled in the pickup's

window rack, let loose
a blast like the trumpet

at Last Judgment,
flinching slightly.

+++

Morphine-shrouded
face in its cold corral

of titanium, rising to a tilted
metal nimbus so like a

broken halo. The mind
such an evil master

at times and death a
double entendre.

Surgeons speak of the
reanimation possible

with purse-string sutures
and parietal bone grafts.

+++

In the creek
crayfish scuttle in

muddy retreat,
frogs chirk at a small

blond boy who bends
to pick a yellow skull

of mushroom. Even now
I hope he recalls

the still creek water,
butterflies wavering

toward the wet throats
of zinnias in sunshine.

Third Place, Patty Dickson Pieczka, Carbondale, IL

Medieval Statue

She's lived in these ruins long enough
for her stone lips to soften.

Frosted shadows melt from her hair;
years crumble, one by one, to her toes.

She's watched witches start fires
from spit and walk through the flames

while the hunger moon cracked its jawbone
on cat's-eye shells and rocks;

she's stood silently through ribs of famine,
bagpipe howl, leers of plundering gallowglass,

seen the souls of townsfolk rise
in the fog of Loch Lomond,

felt a thousand copper dreams
plummet to the hollows of this old stone well.

DONALD STODGHILL MEMORIAL AWARD, CONTEST 6 (ANY SUBJECT)

First Place, Barbara Blanks, Garland, TX

We're Not Going to Disneyland

Because I could not stop for Death—
He kindly stopped for me—
The Carriage held but just Ourselves—
And Immortality.
~ Emily Dickinson

Because I could not stop for Death—
he is *so* exasperating
wanting my cooperation—
I tried again procrastinating
by creating aggravation.
Because I could not stop for Death

he kindly stopped for me.
Oh, go away, I hissed,
Vamoose, amscray, and shoo!
But he would not desist—
my time was long past due.
He kindly stopped for me.

The carriage held but just ourselves—
plus iPhones, and two Starbucks frapps
with extra whip, a high-def screen-
in-screen TV, plus Google maps
to Heaven, Hell—and stops between.
The carriage held but just ourselves

and Immortality.
For Death knew all the tricks:
that getting there was half
the fun, and full of kicks.
I sure got the last laugh—
and immortality.

DONALD STODGHILL MEMORIAL AWARD, Contest 6 (Any Subject)
Second Place, Kathy Lohrum Cotton, Anna, IL

A Few Slow Winter Bees

Tillie is disappearing:
threadbare edges of her spare frame
scumbled beneath bleached cotton,

wisps of white hair haloed against
her pillow, the spindly filaments
that tether her here—

a teaspoon of food, sip of water,
an unfinished sentence—
unraveling into moonlight.

Her thin voice hovers
close to colorless lips
like a few slow winter bees.

I lean close to listen, nudge near
on the bed's edge, my unintentional
touch answered only by her moan.

From thin skin torn, a startling rosebud
blossoms on the white sheet,
blood-red petals calling to the bees.

DONALD STODGHILL MEMORIAL AWARD, Contest 6 (Any Subject)

Third Place, Christine Irving, Denton, TX

Rendezvous on Ithaca

The Med lies flat today, dull blue plane
stretching beyond the dusty olive tree,
a crumbling harbor wall, into infinite sky.
By midday, ubiquitous old men, transposable
as coins rubbed thin between thick fingers,
forsake their sun-glazed waterfront, sheltering
from light that bleaches every color white.

Firm footsteps startle heat-doped pigeons into flight.
Their clapping wings could raise the dead, but not
a curtain twitches, every soul lost to slumber,
gossip switchboard closed for the siesta.

We do not touch in public, nor gaze; our arms swing
freely back and forth between us, but I anticipate
how light, filtering past blue shutters,
falls in gentle stripes across coarse cotton sheets
turning dusky skin to tiger.

Climbing the steep village street, your golden
wedding ring shrugs sunlight from its shoulder,
flickers like a beacon sending cautionary signals
to careless travelers venturing on foreign seas,
warning them off unexpected dangers inherent
in deep waters and sudden summer storms.

GEORGIA POETRY SOCIETY AWARD, Contest 7 (The American South)
First Place, Lorraine Jeffery, Orem, UT

Saved

New experience for me, away from my ochre hills.
    Children here have never seen snow.
Humidity as smothering as a fleece blanket with
    Spanish moss swinging to and fro.

I eat brisket, beans, rice and catfish,
    food is different, but it's fine.
People here talk of God comfortably and chat
    in the grocery store line,

explain why calling a group of women *you guys*
    doesn't make as much sense as *y'all*.
And my Yankee ears quickly adjust to the soft
    rhythmic lilt of a southern drawl.

In the café, I notice him going from one
    table to another,
then I hear the question—always the same.
    Are you saved, brother?

People smile, answer *yes*, and go back to
    talking and eating,
This could escalate, I think and my Northern
    heart's rapidly beating.

Have you been saved? he asks again.
    Nope, grins a man dressed in black.
Momentarily, the missionary stops and
    then he smiles back.

Well, you should be. He moves on and I have
    a realization—
no whispered comments, no one hustled out,
    no break in conversation.

A sigh issues from my dry mouth,
and I realize, *This is the South.*

GEORGIA POETRY SOCIETY AWARD, CONTEST 7 (THE AMERICAN SOUTH)

Second Place, Judith Tullis, Indian Head Park, IL

Georgia Bite

Between Brunswick and Savannah,
the coastline is dented as if a great
sea monster has bitten off a chunk.

The Georgia Bite fools hurricanes
ridin' north on the Gulf Stream,
makes 'em bypass the barrier islands
which kept Momma sad on St. Simons
'cause she loved hurricanes. She loved
'em so much she named my brother
Windy and my sister Sandy.

Standin' hopeful on the porch
wavin' a hankie at Edna and Hazel in '54,
Connie and Diane in '55,
she felt nothin' but a stiff breeze
and a few raindrops.

Until Dora in '60—
a she-storm not abidin' the rule—
swirled inland thrillin' Momma
who ran down the pier leanin' into the wind
like a ski jumper goin' for the gold.

Before the storm surge could sweep
her into the shippin' channel
us three grabbed Momma and ran her upstairs
waitin' it out behind the storm shutters.

When the howlin' stopped
we crept down soggy stairs to see
how Dora had rearranged our furniture
but all Momma saw was blue crabs,
big as shovels, layin' on the livin' room floor.

Y'all look what that ole girl left us—
crab cakes for a week.

GEORGIA POETRY SOCIETY AWARD, Contest 7 (The American South)
Third Place, Geraldine Felt, Layton, UT

Saint Simons Island, Georgia
Circa 1943–1945

Even the sounds
in the island's name
conjure precious memories:

>   glint of southern sun
>   winking off waves splashing
>   against miles of white sand
>   our daily dip in the tepid sea
>   nighttime strolls around
>   a darkened lighthouse
>   fishing off a rickety old pier
>   that squeaks and chatters
>   with us when we cross
>   skinny-tired bicycle jaunts
>   on winding roads shaded by forest
>   of live-oaks dripping with Spanish moss.

The small, over a garage, war-time
apartment we called home and
our childless, aging landlord and wife
who gathered us in and treated us like their own
by including us at dinner parties, where we
experienced renowned Southern hospitality.

The huge silver blimp hovering over the island,
vigilant in its watch for enemy submarines,
helped us feel more secure—
but was a constant reminder that
the Saint Simons Naval Air Base
specialized in maintenance of a secret weapon
that the enemy coveted, and that our charming

    island is a vulnerable place connected
    to the mainland with ten worn wooden bridges.

Looking back, I understood well enough that
throughout the warring world, men lay wounded,
dying and that my darling sailor may ship out any day.
But we were newlyweds, deeply in love and young enough
to feel full of hope—almost invincible as we pushed
worries aside and tried to live one joyful day at a time.

POETRY SOCIETY OF TEXAS AWARD, CONTEST 8 (ANY SUBJECT)
First Place, Terry Miller, Richmond, TX

A Whisper in Dime Box*

I am soul pilgrim to his holy place
of mud and cow dung. Spring's complacent sun
suspends above waving usher pines
on the west edge my brother's pasture.
Cattle know my gait and rank, dismissing
my presence as no threat to newborn calves.

Here breathing is simple as religion.
The congregation accepts life's cold weight
and knows its burdens not as punishment
but as time's immediate circumstance.
There is no judging. There are no stones cast.
There are only the hymns: bird, wind and peace.

A watchful mother permits her daughter
to stumble slowly toward my outstretched hand.
Large, dark eyes study and quickly accept
what the bovine mind cannot understand—
the gaunt mystery of two-legged-ness
and smell of soap tinged with sudden sadness.

How my brother loved these amiable creatures;
their smell, the texture of their dusty hides.
We stood in this very place last winter
when he prophesied life's soon arrival,
not knowing as one entered, one would leave.
His full heart failed to see him through to spring.

Now the calf has something new to puzzle
as I confess my emptiness to her.
I release grief from my heart's taut halter.
Mockingbirds have a fresh solemn song to learn
about a broken sibling's loneliness
that echoes over hushed dandelion and thistle.

The cattle slip west so slowly that I
didn't notice our travel toward the trees.
Brother's spirit whispers, *it's time to move on.*

*Dime Box is a small town in southeast Texas

POETRY SOCIETY OF TEXAS AWARD, Contest 8 (Any Subject)
Second Place, Kathy Lohrum Cotton, Anna, IL

Old Poet at the Open Mic

I applaud the passionate angst and anger
of each young reader,
then take my own shaky turn at the mic.

Listen to me, I read softly,
listen, because I am old and know things
you do not yet know.

Louder now, and looking into their eyes:
Listen to me
because I've heard the groan of pulleys
that lower father, mother, husband,
an entire generation of family
into shoveled holes,
       yet am neither lonely, nor alone.

Listen because I've found soaring love
and lost it,
       yet love still, love more.

Listen because this body bears the scars
of scalpels and sickness piled on sickness,
       yet I am well,
because I have retired from jobs
       but never from work,
because I lived through violent storm
and tossed precious things overboard
       but miss none of it.

Listen, because I drowned
       in deep currents of despair,
       yet floated back to sunlight.

Listen to me, I whisper into the mic,
       listen to me,
because I am old and know things
your young hearts could know.

POETRY SOCIETY OF TEXAS AWARD, CONTEST 8 (ANY SUBJECT)

Third Place, Beth Staas, Oak Brook, IL

Family Album

His clothes match the desert drab,
his smile uncertain and brave,
a twenty-something off to war.
Even his signature is cheerful,
To Gram, from Johnny.

There's another Johnny.
With helmet bobbing,
he joined men aboard ship
to fight on foreign soil
in the good war.
Then another signature,
To Sis, now her soldier boy.

It's all that remains.

Other pages yellow into sepia,
faces proud, strong, determined,
heads held high,
Uncle Otto, Uncle John,
my own father, all soldier boys
in a war to end all wars,
and a simple note that says
We are all brothers,

all gone.

It should have been
All Quiet on the Western Front,
and peace in our time.
Instead, it was freezing cold,
blazing heat, mud and sand,
while boys screamed for their mothers
before dying.

Pictures can lie.

THE CHILDREN'S HOUR, CONTEST 9 (POETRY FOR CHILDREN)

First Place, Harvey Stone, Johnson City, TN

The Drop

It was chilly and windy the day I was born.
Some say I came from the eye of the storm.
Falling so fast, with others around,
I feared what would happen when I hit the ground.
When I finally splash-landed, for I had no brake,
I found myself safely in the middle of a lake.
I asked what would happen, now I was here,
"Do raindrops live on? Do we ever disappear?"
Two fates are possible, here in the lake,
either travel down river, or evaporate.
"What do you mean? Poof I am gone?
Where would I go? It's here I belong."
The way of the river, that's how I'll go,
a journey downstream, just riding the flow.
I was well on my way, halfway to the sea,
when a pipe and pump grabbed a strong hold on me.
Swept away fast, forced through miles of duct,
then pushed through a faucet into a cup.
A boy picked me up and I went down in the drink
from belly to bloodstream, quick as a wink.
He rushed out the door and ran up the street.
I came out as sweat running down his red cheek.
I fell on hot blacktop, and poof I was gone,
evaporated to nothing, into the beyond.
But wait. I'm still here. I've not gone you will see.
I just shed my droplet. I'm now floating free.
Back in the air, not visible by eye.
I will someday reappear as a cloud in the sky.
Then I will fall once again to the earth.
For this is my cycle of continued rebirth.

THE CHILDREN'S HOUR, Contest 9 (Poetry for Children)

Second Place, Kolette Montague, Centerville, UT

Flower Power

If I could make a daisy chain
and wrap it 'round my friends,
then each of them continued it
with friends and friends and friends,

our chain would hug the whole wide world
and soon, I know we'd find
that every person held a link,
with no one left behind.

The daisies' circle round the world
would make a chain of friends
where all could live in harmony
and peace that never ends.

THE CHILDREN'S HOUR, Contest 9 (Poetry for Children)

Third Place, Jerri Hardesty, Brierfield, AL

Wild Party

One summer day, in mid-July,
We hung the family wash out to dry,
Then went inside away from hot sun—
But the animals thought they'd have some fun.
The silly goose began to clown,
The donkey pushed a fence post down,
So cows got out and pigs did, too,
To run around and squeal and moo.
The goats and sheep escaped their pen
And roused and ruffled every hen,
The dogs and cats joined in the play
With chickens' squawks and donkey's bray.
They pulled the laundry from the line,
Some got yours, some got mine,
We found them there, this story goes,
All dressed up in people clothes.

AL LASTER MEMORIAL AWARD, CONTEST 10 (AN EKPHRASTIC POEM)

First Place, Amy Irish, Lakewood, CO

The Winged Nike (of Nevada)

He throws the goddess a poker chip.

We are touring my father's favorite foreign country—
Las Vegas, Nevada. Here stands an America
As counterfeiter, re-printing the cultural currency
Of the world. Handing out the funny money
With one hand, All You Can Eat fliers with the other.

Here stands a younger sister of the statue, a lesser deity
Still jealous of her famous older sibling, resentful
Of time she never had working the Mediterranean scene.
This version stands above a motionless, man-made sea—
"Fountain broken, sorry for the inconvenience."

Here, her flawless robes billow
In the breeze of a thousand
Smokers exhaling.

This pale echo of the Paris Nike leaves me
Aching. Remembering how she crested
Like crashing surf on the prow
Of a stone ship, seeming to alight
There in the Louvre a moment before.

Remembering her wings spread, flush
As sails. Remembering how she summoned
The Aegean winds to sweep me with her
Out to sea. Remembering the arc and flex
Of her muscles, calling out Alive, Alive, Alive….

Here, commandments against graven images
Are conveniently forgotten, and every temple
Resurrected. Here, there is a feast of false gods.

But there is still worship for her, outside these churches
Of chance. Still the gratitude and gifts; the pleas

And prayers. And I still feel her power
Knocking me to my knees. Even in this phony oasis
I am cracked open, receiving her glory.

Here, her fractured form leads a crooked congregation
In AA prayers. One meeting for each
Of this city's sins. And all with ample coffee.

This American Goddess leads a new religion—the holy path
Of piecing ourselves together from the ruins. Her belief—
That the broken can still be beautiful. Her blessing—a Victory
For every inner war. To Her I pray I'll rise from my own ashes.
If I win, I'll follow my father's lead—and tip the Goddess, too.

Surreally Good Apple

This is Not an Apple (and *The Treachery of Images*,
aka *This is Not a Pipe*) by Rene Magritte

While waiting for Magritte in his garden studio,
I pluck an apple from a canvas
and eat it.

Magritte enters and sees me devouring the apple,
beside a freshly unpainted canvas, and shouts
about how that *image* was clearly marked
not an *apple*!

I didn't see that. It just looked delicious
and it was.

He points to a pipe and tries to explain
the *treachery of images*.

What treachery? All I see is a pipe I could
reach out and touch, so I pick it up
and light it.

Magritte stares blankly at me and the second
emptied canvas. "Do you know how long
it took me to create that apple? That pipe?"

"It's just that you're so good," I say.
"These were so real, but I don't *get*
the other stuff," I admit, with a puff,
and ask him to explain.

"It's all *surreal*," he answers
with a broad, sweeping stroke.
"Well," I say, "the apple and pipe
are *so real*, but the rest, I *really* don't get."

"It's all *surreal*," he repeats, waving his paintbrush,
spraying the room with applesauce and ash,
spinning in the space of impossible portraits
and wild absurdities, apples, clouds, boulders
floating without the slightest care for reality
or the serious nature of gravity, "Surreal!
Surreal! It's all surreal."

"Okay, it's *so real*," I agree, to be polite,
adding, "Maybe it's me. I don't *get* a lot of art."

But the apple and the pipe
I enjoyed immensely.

AL LASTER MEMORIAL AWARD, CONTEST 10 (AN EKPHRASTIC POEM)

Third Place, Robin Gow, Mineola, NY

flowers 1964
after Andy Warhol

the girl i loved's name was orange.
we ate flowers made of fuchsia.
biting the walls, they turned primrose.
our favorite planet was red.
the morning turned the house white.

the girl i loved's name was fuchsia.
we hated flowers, all of them primrose.
plucking them until our fingers were red.
the stems of the flowers died white.
in the kitchen we split an orange.

the girl i loved's name was primrose.
we dyed each other in rivers, came out red.
the inside of apples is white
& so is the underbelly of an orange.
we ran away & called all the towns fuchsia.

the girl i loved's name was red.
she liked strawberries unripe & white.
we dipped our fingers in sun-yolk orange
& swallowed it; the sky tasted fuchsia.
she told me life's not a primrose.

the girl i loved's name was white.
why didn't she like the color orange?
she would paint canvases entirely fuchsia.
undressing me, she'd laugh you're so primrose.
we'd bite off the other's lips, kiss red.

FLORIDA STATE POETS ASSOCIATION, INC. AWARD, CONTEST 11 (SUBJECT: FLORIDA)

First Place, Micki Blenkush, St. Cloud, MN

Riding the Down and Up Waves
Shell Key Shuttle, St. Pete Beach, Florida

We arrive early to catch the first ferry,
the shuttle's captain, sun-baked and weary-patient,
tells us where and how to wait.
One guy snaps, *The line starts over here,*
while another peppers his response
with *Buddy* in the way of one decidedly not.
These will be our people: mirrored
sunglasses, torn away shirt sleeves,
bickering couples staring into their phones,
and a woman who lost her lower jaw
to some kind of surgery.
Ten minutes across the channel,
we skip the line for umbrellas, scurry ahead
for the best selection
of conch, whelks, augers, and scallops.
At the end of the preserve's allowable border
my daughter puts on her goggles
and runs into the waves
where she finds her first and only sand dollar
small and round as the palm of her hand.
While I wait on my towel
in the thin shade of low brush,
someone sneaks a fully intact second
on top of our mesh bag,
a man stops by to hand forth a third,
and, in our swaying line to shuttle back,
the woman without a lower jaw
wordlessly offers another,
its star an etched flower.

FLORIDA STATE POETS ASSOCIATION, INC. AWARD, CONTEST 11 (SUBJECT: FLORIDA)
Second Place, Janet Watson, Wesley Chapel, FL

The Highest Range

There are no mountains and rarely a hint of hill
pushing up from Florida's flatlands.
Yet, massive shape-changers
move through blue satin sky,
higher than any earthly range.
Creamy mounds float over cypress domes
and green pastures where cattle graze.
Airily suspended, in a way that monoliths
of rock could never be,
they cast their shadows far below.

They storm through summer in menacing gray.
Bulging with seawater they race over the land
flashing and roaring. All day long they will
carry Atlantic seawater westward,
from one side of the peninsula to the other,
pouring it out over land, with hardly
a drop left to drip into the Gulf.
But a soft silhouette against the sky
remains, a blanket to pull over the sun
and put the day to sleep.

On another morning, pale promises appear,
which take all of a day to build into summits.
Only hawks climb these heights,
soaring and circling, polishing the peaks.
Driven by great air currents that come
from places we have never seen,
the mountains lift higher and higher,
out of reach, even to the birds.
We, anchored to earth, gaze at them
and believe that this must surely be
the Heaven where God lives.

FLORIDA STATE POETS ASSOCIATION, INC. AWARD, CONTEST 11 (SUBJECT: FLORIDA)

Third Place, Doris Jones, Madison, MS

Beachside Jazz
a Gulf thunderstorm, hotel-view

The thrumming surf counts off,
beats time on sand—
a pulsing-deep rhythm,
the foamy heartbeat
called from ocean's core.

Caught up in the music,
a syncopation of sand
scrunch-slides
to uncover new wonders,
reveal its treasures.

Palm trees gyrate,
fronds snap, keeping time
with the wailing-sax wind.
They lean in, lean out,
transported by the beat.

As storm clouds cluster,
the light show's brilliance signals
the finale. Thunder claps,
and sweet music rains down,
each drop pits the sand,
leaving its memory.

ALABAMA STATE POETRY SOCIETY AWARD, Contest 12 (Tell Me Something Beautiful)

First Place, Gwen Gunn, Guilford, CT

Found Gift

lilies taken from the church
from many left forgotten
gracefully arch across their window perch
seven flowers and one more bud to open

their fragrance fills the bedroom
tulips and hydrangeas also thrive
nearly two weeks later still in bloom
chosen since they can survive

what pleasure to plan where they might live
if   after flowering   planted in our garden
how fitting an Easter gift you give
though they could be considered stolen

resurrection   is what they bring to mind
saved for rebirth by your find

ALABAMA STATE POETRY SOCIETY AWARD, Contest 12 (Tell Me Something Beautiful)
Second Place, Patricia Barnes, Wyandotte, MI

Napping Baby

She lies in a rounded lump,
blanketed, bundled in soft
pink flannel sprinkled with stars

of yellow and white, while
a music mobile, run out of winding,
turns, silent, over her head
in a quiet carnival.

Think the whisper of dandelion
puffs rising and drifting,
her breath, its own music,

she sleeps the innocence
of peaches and freshwater
springs. Her dreams

are fearless. As if
the angry world were
unreal and her nursery

the whole universe,
stars and all, the milky
way a dribble on her chin.

Imagine we could nap
like this, secure and
treasured more than all

the household goods and
chattels we've amassed and held
as wealth before she came

to touch us with her
little sucking sounds
and the smell of newness
in her skin.

ALABAMA STATE POETRY SOCIETY AWARD, Contest 12 (Tell Me Something Beautiful)
Third Place, John W. Coppock, Tuttle, OK

Reflection

Unlike azaleas
    blazing on the lake
        that slowly fade unfelt
            into the dark
or moonlight
    glancing off the wake behind the boat we rented in the park
    till dawn rekindled color there to take us from ourselves
your touch was known to me.

Like water
    seeping down through porous stone
        to move about the dark interiors of faults no human feels
            but in himself alone,
your silent shape
    eased slowly through the salts
        to leave a hollow
            beautifully grown
                about the stream whose touching made it so.

LAND OF ENCHANTMENT AWARD, Contest 13 (Borders)
First Place, Christian Shute, Cheyenne, WY

King of the Cul de Sac

Merely walking on the sidewalk
When I entered your domain
You came out yelling demands
It was me you tried to detain

I kept on walking away
You decided to pursue me
Though you already called the police
You chose to be a hero wannabe

For you are the King of the Cul de Sac
A self-proclaimed duty to protect
Even an innocent person walking
Becomes a criminal suspect

I do not respect your imagined authority
In fact, I do not respect you
Your belligerent actions and unjustified anger
Made the police see you right through

You were genuinely surprised when the police
Said you could not ban me walking
On a public sidewalk in America
Your ignorance and arrogance are shocking

I was not detained or even frisked
And I was allowed to go on my way
The King of the Cul de Sac was told to go home
His majesty clearly lost that day

LAND OF ENCHANTMENT AWARD, CONTEST 13 (BORDERS)

Second Place, Nancy Breem, Loveland, OH

Virginia Specter

You, a flash of white blouse
at the foot of my bed,
who were you? In a motel
in Lexington, Virginia,
with both Jackson and Lee
resting in graves nearby,
the logical conclusion
would be a Civil War figure,
but there was more gentleman
than soldier about you, that
shirt with the generous sleeves
unlike anything in butternut or blue.

From the way you dashed
around the corner into the bathroom,
I think I startled you as much as you
did me. I never know what ghosts
are up to. You weren't there to scare.
Were you simply watching as I slept,

or did we simultaneously cross borders?
In your world, was I
the ghost who frightened you?

LAND OF ENCHANTMENT AWARD, CONTEST 13 (BORDERS)
Third Place, Maxine Carlson, Iowa City, IA

Note to His New Wife

when he puts his heart
very close to mine
when my feet fly out
in a whirling hug
remember we met
decades before you

energetic twirls
remind my husband
of exuberant
puppies—he understands
we're almost siblings
we will soon recall
age and location
silence loud laughter
include our spouses

but if he must choose
friend or family
of course he'll pick you
the love of his life

though forever after
he'll like me just the
same
like you a little less
and *I won't like you at all*

THE VIRGINIA CORRIE-COZART MEMORIAL AWARD, Contest 14 (Art and Artistry)

First Place, Claudia Van Gerven, Boulder, CO

When the Trees Escaped

Sometime in the midst of the 19th century, the trees
got loose, their shadows turned blue. They were
no longer content to line the lake in umbers, in olive,
wouldn't settle for limpid reflections
congealing on the surface. They wanted to shake
and shimmy like flappers absolved of bustles, of corsets,
like holy rollers reborn in hallelujahs of cobalt and puce.

They rose up off the canvas in lush emerald impasto
or tigered in yellow and black, their woody torsos
arching like wrestlers preparing for a match. And all the little
leaves wanted voices, aves of chartreuse, wanted to cheer
lavender skies, explosions of pearly clouds.

Even trees on the banks of the Stour, even proper British trees,
and the cows resting beneath them, lost their brown, beefy
complacency, were struck with the edge
of the palette knife till they hummed with industrial
energy, cleft nostalgia's dogmatic surface, burst out
of the great chain of being.

THE VIRGINIA CORRIE-COZART MEMORIAL AWARD, Contest 14 ((Art and Artistry))
Second Place, Lorrie Wolfe, Windsor, CO

Marks on Paper

*I read and write poetry because it continues to amaze me
how a few dark marks on a piece of paper can bloom into
images and metaphors that question, reveal and gladden
the mystery....* ~Fredrick Zydek

Surely we are more than mere dark marks on paper.
They say what is spoken flies away but
I am haunted by what is written,
the fact of ink,
making permanent the fleeting.

As if the act of marking
could make the thing more real.
But which is the more real?

I remember your smile
and there is no word,
nor *sumie* stroke,
that captures the movement of your hair
that day we stood in the wind,
looking over the bridge rail
at the river flowing below
with our first lovemaking
hanging as still as an un-rung bell
between us, waiting to peal its surprise
and pronounce we are one,
we are one.

THE VIRGINIA CORRIE-COZART MEMORIAL AWARD, Contest 14 ((Art and Artistry)
Third Place, Marleine Yanish, Denver, CO

Becoming Music

I'm on an arc
adrift between levels

Were am I
                not?

Though my body
lays in bed
I wake but not

wonder

                still

I was listening to music
became the music

no form
yet in form
                still

still

vibrating formless
As glass turns
to sand and back

ARIZONA STATE POETRY SOCIETY AWARD, Contest 15 (Borrowed Books)

First Place, Robert E. Blenheim, Daytona Beach, FL

A Wet Dream in a Dry Season

In the middle of a starless night
a young woman is nearly done disrobing.
After a day of smearing rivers of color on an unfinished canvas
she collapses on her bed, and with an air of defiance kicks off
the last remaining article of her clothing, a left sandal
which makes a softened thud as it lands on the Persian rug.
A tub of steaming clean water in the next room beckons to her
and hearing its call she rises, stretches, tilts sideways
to let her nude body leisurely lean against a mahogany bookcase.
She allows her right hand to drift up, letting its index finger
randomly select a particular gold-embossed library book
that she had once checked out and forgot to return:
A lusciously bound volume of my own collected poems.

She makes a promise.
Never having even cracked open its covers, she vows
that after her body emerges clean from the healing sudsy waters
that will caress her flesh like a thousand lovers' kisses,
she will drop this book on her bed, let it fly open to any page fate decides.
Then reclining naked over the page she will read it aloud to herself,
taking its words in as her many pores had taken the luxurious heat in.

But, alas, the water manages to cleanse her mind as well as her body
so she forgets about the book, forgets about her honest vow.
She goes about her life, moves away to another city, another world,
takes on one lover and then another, all to fade even in a dream's vision.

Now awake I am moved to finish the dream.
Eventually married, she lives to an old age, her husband dies, now alone.
Maybe before she dies she'll finally open the book and read.
Or maybe she won't.

Even if she never knows,
even before I had this dream,
even before I wrote my first poem,
maybe even before I was born,
she had been the one for whom I wrote everything.

ARIZONA STATE POETRY SOCIETY AWARD, CONTEST 15 (BORROWED BOOKS)
Second Place, Julie Shavin, Fountain, CO

Judging the Cover

We are not reading and wish we were.
In this house of letters, we fake our themes.

Our final home, final windows
open to fields from which the horses
have been withdrawn. The wind slithers
in small and stunted trees.
This is our default life, and we know it.

How we wish we were reading this story.
At 4 you begin drinking, saying,
it's not the middle of the day, after all,
and it is not, although you rose at noon.
At 6 I join you.
The boredom of the prairie is old age's love-child,
but we hope something will happen.

We are one another's fictions,
have taken all we needed, cannot give back.

We belong to those not in our story,
those who have gone,
who will always be our story.
We are overdue happiness, and at times,
have an inkling: we laugh at the silly dog,
cross-pet the cats on our laps,
think, *it isn't really so bad.*

Charade becomes a new day,
and we're hoping the wind will shift,
the dead will rise, and the heavens resound
with some unexpected chapter.
On and on we read, impossibly,
turning, turning, just in case.

Never Land Sixty-Six Years Later:

*The Thousand Word Sequel
Conveyed by Picture of Old Man
Hovering Above the Ground
Balanced on One Hand on a Beer Bottle*

When Peter Pan had called it quits
with Neverland, survived the blitz
in London and the austere life
that followed it with English wife,
he and his shadow parted ways
again. His shadow longed for days
of timeless youth on tropic isle,
and Peter reveled for a while
in growing (which he'd never done)
without a dark side in the sun.
Somehow, though, growing turned to age
as decades swept across the stage
the world became. Now grown, he shrank,
And could fly only when he drank.

MILDRED VORPAHL BAASS REMEMBRANCE AWARD, Contest 16 (Domestic Cats)

First Place, Cynthia Nankee, Canton, MI

(Not Quite) Still Life in the Garden: Black Cat with Pumpkins

I am the black,
keeping watch over large buds
of orange.

I wait for faces: Cheshire grins…
eyes that will pierce the dark
hood of night.

I have moved with a whisper
to settle down at this spot. For, I am as
graceful as yesterday's leaf—

transferred by
        the invisible wind.

MILDRED VORPAHL BAASS REMEMBRANCE AWARD, CONTEST 16 (DOMESTIC CATS)

Second Place, Robert Schinzel, Highland Village, TX

If Winter Comes…

Purring from behind a stack of lumber
at the local hardware store,
a calico cat comes forward, weaves
a dance around my ankles, whispers
its way from stray to homesteader.

The cottonwoods show a faint hint of fall
in late September, a good month of the year
before winter comes, a good name
for a creature joining our clan.
She takes to the farm outside of town
as if born to bond with a family.
The kids bring September inside at night
where she chooses different beds for sleeping.
Weeks pass in routine, till her disappearance.
We fear the worst, roadway accident, coyote.

A few days later, shouts come
from our son's bedroom closet.
Curled in the corner of a dresser drawer
among socks and underwear,
like a pile of rustling autumn leaves,
September lies nursing
October, November and December.
Behind some folded sweaters, we find
February crawling past January.
We wonder, can March be far behind?

MILDRED VORPAHL BAASS REMEMBRANCE AWARD, CONTEST 16 (DOMESTIC CATS)

Third Place, Carol Williams, York, PA

Long-Haired Cat

He has left lumps of softness here and there,
so much orange fur along his feline route
room to room, couch to chair to ottoman,
I sometimes expect to see him sidling in
as simply skeleton, ivory knobs and tubes
assembled in random slinky fashion:
cat castanets, lizardy knuckles,
scrimshaw arches of shoulders
and backbent knees, the green orbs
of his merciless eyes bulging
around slant pupils as he makes
his subtle intercostal way with light
shining through ribs and larynx,
lifting his feet delicately like
a ballet dancer walking through tar,
and his purr rattling like bean seeds
inside a hollow skull.

LEAGUE OF MINNESOTA POETS AWARD, CONTEST 17 (FREE VERSE)
First Place, Rita Geil, Carson City, NV

Directions for Daughters

Be the beginning.

Fill your arms with a flowering constellation.
Invite the souls of unborn songbirds.
Shake the glass trees and listen.

Run your hands softly over your life.
Feel the loose, bright fabric of your breath.
Dance your story.

Find the source of the fountain.
Let nothing distract you.
Follow your soul on the silver spiral.
Wear the twilight like a length of indigo satin.

LEAGUE OF MINNESOTA POETS AWARD, CONTEST 17 (FREE VERSE)
Second Place, Diane Glancy, Gainesville, TX

A Night on the Lake

Northern Lights are a forest
    of moving pines
        trapped in the earth's magnetic field.

    Northern Lights are charged particles
that arrive on the tongue of solar winds.

Northern Lights are jungle animals
    transported to earth
    pacing back and forth in their cages.

      Northern Lights are bulldozers that
  shape and align the sky
shifting as the moon moving on the water.

Northern Lights are fishing boats rocking
    on the waves.

Northern Lights are scouts that bivouac near the shore.
    By morning
        they pick up and travel on.

LEAGUE OF MINNESOTA POETS AWARD, CONTEST 17 (FREE VERSE)

Third Place, Barbara Blanks, Garland, TX

Out for Blood

Vampires
              soooooo romantic
hugme kissme biteme

kissing bugs   mosquitoes
   leeches
     fleas   bedbugs
ticks hookworms

      blood suckers Unite!

bare-chested   bodice-busting
    seductive   secretive
crawlers of night   dark desires
     here's my throat   my arms
my *et cetera et cetera et* —
             wrap around my body
take me take me   oh, have at me
   lordy   Lordy   LORDY!

I am prey
     pray for us sinners
        prey on me
   killer whale   wolf of the sea
    seize me   eat me
werewolf   beware the wolf
  wolf at the door   come in come in
     bare me
   bear   with me
       menu: berries   fish   me
dragged from my tent
   I am a food source

Did you get the memo on
     how superior humans are?

JESSICA C. SAUNDERS MEMORIAL AWARD, CONTEST 18 (FORM: VILLANELLE)

First Place, Charmaine Pappas Donovan, Brainerd, MN

Storm Phobia

While fists of thunder rumble, blacken skies,
a tempest wakes to clear its gurgling throat.
Winds shriek through trees, shake windows with their cries.

Bright zigzag lightens clouds disguised as spies.
Rain falls in slanted arrows, nature's rote.
While fists of thunder rumble, blackened skies

resume their march, bass drums monotonize.
I cross my heart, vow to remain remote.
Winds shriek through trees, shake windows with their cries.

I lied. My vow dissolves in tears, I rise
to wave my flag. Give up. Write final note.
While fists of thunder rumble, blacken skies,

I fall into my fear. Dark magnifies.
Unmoored, will my boat sink, or stay afloat?
Winds shriek through trees, shake windows with their cries.

I promise—hands on ears—I will devise
a sure-fire cure: a storm-fear antidote.
while fists of thunder rumble, blacken skies,
winds shriek through trees, shake windows with their cries.

JESSICA C. SAUNDERS MEMORIAL AWARD, Contest 18 (Form: Villanelle)
Second Place, Wendy Visser, Cambridge, Ontario

Adrift

For those who see dark in the light of day,
caught in the clutch of our verdict's dead stare;
so convinced they say, there's no other way.

For those who fall short of the sun's warm spray,
a backpack called home is filled with despair,
for those who see dark in the light of day.

So downtrodden down by life's sad display,
sleeping on benches, no blankets to wear;
so convinced they say, there's no other way.

Needs are simple on the signs they portray,
and life off the streets just doesn't compare,
for those who see dark in the light of day.

From family and friends they often stray,
far too afraid of requests for repair;
so convinced they say, there's no other way.

They firmly believe they're doing okay,
and they bravely bear condemnation's glare.
For those who see dark in the light of day,
so convinced they say, there's no other way.

JESSICA C. SAUNDERS MEMORIAL AWARD, CONTEST 18 (FORM: VILLANELLE)
Third Place, Jana Bouma, Madison Lake, MN

Postponement

I read to you each morning and each night.
Your thrashing feet and grasping hands grow still.
Passion subsides into quiet delight.

Your small voice trembles. Your eyes blink but can't quite
hold back the tears. I rock you, and then—will
I read to you? Each morning and each night,

the words, my voice, the pages put to flight
small troubles, harder griefs, until I feel
passion subside. Into quiet delight

we sink together. How soon will you break
the bonds that hold you on my lap until
I read to you each morning? And each night,

I'll feel your shoulder press against my arm
only for years. I will not get my fill.
But passion subsides into quiet delight

this moment, as you tell me that you might
like one more story. And so, just this while,
I read to you each morning and each night.
Passion subsides into quiet delight.

POETRY SOCIETY OF INDIANA, Contest 19 (Community)

First Place, Beth Staas, Oak Brook, IL

Worship

A simple room, white on white,
a dais in front, burnished from frequent use.
Tinted windows send prisms of light dancing distortions,
while chairs tall and haughty advise leaders how to behave.
A fly flails the wall with a frantic buzz
while ceiling fans measure the beat.
Then it's prayer time, and shoes scrape the wooden floor,
backs shifting against pews, against one another.
Some close their eyes, closeting thoughts, breathing as one.
A final cough, and the air throbs into stillness
to pulse with the Infinite, for this is holy ground.

POETRY SOCIETY OF INDIANA, Contest 19 (Community)
Second Place, Diane Glancy, Gainesville, TX

Yellowtail Lanes, Lodge Grass, Montana

The first time he rolled a ball down the alley
it struck the pins that stood like obstacles—
and they fell down.
Some of them anyway.
And here came his ball rolling back
out of the chute like a gopher from its hole
and he rolled again.

Now the bowling ball was a prairie dog returning
through the chute. A raccoon. Opossum, Fox.
He himself was on a roll.
He joined the bowling club.

Now he was a wolf howling at the round moon
of the ball—Ahhhhooooooooooo.
He named the ten pins—Uncle Bill, Cody, Chase,
Mr. Fouse—the math teacher, Poncho, Rooney,
Cam, Blaze, Orval, Mr. Z.

The bowling balls stampeded down the alley.
It was a buffalo hunt. It was migration.
All the clatter. All the noise.
He knew the terms—Strike. Spare. Fence post.
Mule ears. 7/10 split. He'd done them all.

The bowling alley was named for
Hawk with the Yellow Tail Feathers (1903–1993),
a Crow medicine man and Sun Dancer
whose name was changed to Thomas Yellowtail
for the purpose of assimilation
and to shorten Indian names on U.S. records.

At Yellowtail Lanes the old days rise.
Those left out, overlooked, join the bowling club
and roll their bowling balls
down the lanes one after another—
spare, strike, 7/10 split—
until the lanes blaze with streaks of yellow light.

POETRY SOCIETY OF INDIANA, Contest 19 (Community)

Third Place, Laurie Kolp, Beaumont, TX

Community Comes Out in Troubled Times

After Harvey flooded us out, our town
lost its water supply, stopped faucets.

We boiled tubbed water, waded through brown
after Harvey flooded us out (our town

a mud-muck mess), bathed in neighbors' pools, sounds
of helicopter hums amongst our chats.

After Harvey flooded us out, our town
lost its water supply, not our spirit.

First Place, Tony Fusco, West Haven, CT

The Flag Is Upside Down

In the twilight of America
when all the lights went out
        there was no rapture
but there were bodies in the sky,
when cities drowned
        the wheat fields shriveled
            the orchards dried up,
where books were barred
        books were burned
            books were left unread,
where no news was true news
when the eyes of the people glazed over
        the ears waxed full,
where dead diseases
        returned from the grave,
when the churches were closed
        the pews already empty.
The earth shook
        the mud slid
            lightning filled the skies
like skeleton hands. When the wind twisted
        its whirlwind breaking great buildings,
when the towers fell,
        when wildfires ate the landscape.

In the twilight of America
crowds fought in the parks
        with clubs and rocks and torches.
In the twilight of America
when everyone carried rifle on a sling
        a handgun in their handbags
when children hid under desks in lockdown
        and runners blew to bits in the street.
In the twilight of America
the flag already hung at half mast
lowered the rest of the way down.

NEVADA POETRY SOCIETY AWARD, CONTEST 20 (POLITICS)
Second Place, Paula J. Lambert, Dublin, OH

Siege
for TJ Garrett

We need to make a collective word,
she said, for the number of women
it takes to make our claims of violence
believable: an exultation of larks,
a watch of nightingales, a siege of women
who aren't taking shit anymore.

Exultation, watch, siege. We are songbirds
turned to birds of prey: an unkindness,
a scream, a gang, a posse, a murder.
We're a mustering, a wake, a stand,
a clutch, a clattering, a congress. We're
a congregation, a new religion: Divine.
Dreadful. Celestial. Bestial. We are
the Creator. The Destroyer. The Mastermind.
We are troublemakers, agitators, instigators,
leaders. We are the majority.

We need to make a collective word,
she said, for the number of women it takes
to make our claims believable: an exultation,
a watch, a siege. A vote of women. A canvass.
A consult. A block, a ballot, a win. A victory
of women. A triumph. A conquest.
A landslide.

NEVADA POETRY SOCIETY AWARD, Contest 20 (Politics)

Third Place, Gail Denham, Sunriver, OR

Items I Read Last Year

*after "Things I Learned Last Week"
by William Stafford*

A minuscule frog in Klamath County
brought irrigation to a halt; nearby
farmland dried up.

Sometimes mother dogs nurse
orphaned squirrels along with her pups.

A swash-buckling politician will come
to your university for half a million
dollars and tell you how to stay humble.

Beethoven was deaf, yet he wrote
intricate symphonies from the music
that endlessly bounced inside his head.

If I'm allowed to live more years, I want
to be loving and aware of everyone around
me, drink good coffee; sing and dance
around the kitchen like a six-year-old.

In government offices, three staplers,
two packets of printer paper, five ballpoint pens,
and four boxes of paper clips cost tax
payers as much as their weekly grocery bill.

WILLIAM STAFFORD MEMORIAL AWARD, Contest 21 (Any Subject)

First Place, LaVern Spencer McCarthy, Blair, OK

The Old, Yellow School Bus

A yellow bus meanders up the lane
with thirty children singing on and on.
My hound dog howls. He loves a good refrain.
A swirl of dust remains when they are gone.

With thirty children singing on and on,
the driver waves and gives a happy smile.
A swirl of dust remains when they are gone,
the old behemoth creaking all the while.

The driver waves and gives a happy smile
as dreams of home take all his cares away,
the old behemoth creaking all the while.
His route is almost finished for the day.

As dreams of home take all his cares away,
the driver sighs and thinks of years gone by.
His route is almost finished for the day.
He wishes that big rattle trap could fly.

The driver sighs and thinks of years gone by.
Retirement nears. His working days are few.
He wishes that big rattle trap could fly.
He drove the bus when it was bright and new.

Retirement nears. His working days are few,
but he will miss the laughter and the joy.
He drove the bus when it was bright and new,
a happy ride for every girl and boy.

But he will miss the laughter and the joy.
My hound dog howls. He loves a good refrain.
A happy ride for every girl and boy,
a yellow bus meanders up the lane.

Cancer

My body is an oil rig.
Inside flammable liquid
safe for now a protected
embryo until one cell
goes rogue one tire skids
and all raw goods and crude
tumble, spill onto concrete.
My lymph nodes are highways
of toxicity, my scars, railroad
tracks. My veins contain
fierce semis loaded with
germs and poison and fumes.
Their convoys are pink skin
beaten down by wave
after wave of radiation.

When I accelerate, drive blindly
towards the next infusion,
my port providing navigation
as I move past the intersection
of chemicals and confession,
I see my life like a freighter
before my eyes, and I pick up
the CB radio, wildly try to connect
with anybody with everybody
until I remember not to fill up
on the wrong kind of fuel,
but instead to lean closer
to Love and let the wind
whisper its prayer.

WILLIAM STAFFORD MEMORIAL AWARD, CONTEST 21 (ANY SUBJECT)
Third Place, Catherine Moran, Little Rock, AR

All the forgotten pieces

Sometimes when I play golf, I feel a twinge
of guilt because I haven't used one club
in quite a while. And so I stop and pull
my five iron out and give the ball a whack
as if that stick had pent-up feelings like
a child not chosen for a team. I have
a pair of tennis shoes that do not match
so many clothes and when I get them out
I watch a smile and quickened breath appear.
They step more lively as they see the light
again and prance around the room with me.
I feel a little sorry for a knife
of longtime use that lies behind a stack
of brighter ones. Deliberately I pick
it out and listen to that swish and snap
at squash and cucumbers and apples too.
I know it feels important to be used.

I bet that most of us can readily
recall a teacher choosing someone else
to dust erasers or give out some books.
But hopefully we got our turn to help
instead of wilting like a quiet fern
in back of rows of loud geraniums.

It's not as if I don't give time and thought
to those neglected persons waiting in
the hallways of our lives. Those wistful eyes
can stir complacent feelings quicker than
a Mozart symphony. A friend once said
my savior complex stretched to everything
within the reach of arms and surely hearts.
And now that reach extends beyond my skin
to all the fragile pieces I can choose
to touch. I'll pick for soup that simple bowl
that's hidden on the second shelf and feel
it glow with warmth this wintry afternoon.

THE NEW YORK POETRY FORUM AWARD, Contest 22 (The Art of Poetry)
First Place, Andrea McBride, Wesley Chapel, FL

Writing Outside

I watch an ant maze
its way across the almost

blank page, bumping
up against

my inked ideas
and swirling again

in the white space.

Flight

is given to birds
but not to pilots
or poets, who must learn

to distinguish between
elevators, ailerons,
assonance, alliteration;

who must learn the critical
angle of attack
and how to counteract

a tendency for similes
to stall;
who over years may learn

to widen vision at the edges,
read clouds,
embrace a fickle wind—

if only once
to soar
on words as strong as feathers.

THE NEW YORK POETRY FORUM AWARD, Contest 22 (The Art of Poetry)
Third Place, Robert Schinzel, Highland Village, TX

Whiteout

Alone in the woods I pretend to hunt deer,
my rifle just for appearance. I want to see
if solitude speaks words to me,
words that I can later plagiarize.
Huge flakes, downy feathers of the forest,
float among the trees like discarded paper,
silencing every sound, obscuring every view.
The new-fallen blanket covers my footprints.
My eyes search the trees for north-clinging moss
or the faintest glow of sun, anything to act
as a compass to point the way
toward avenues of escape.

I need something that can look around
tree trunks, see through snow banks,
find the sun, make lines that guide me
in my blindness. Flurries fall ever deeper,
homogenizing the land. I look for color,
for contrast.

Then a fence appears off to my right,
rusted wire and salvation, a guide
to lead me to the road, to escape the barrens.
My spirit soars at the simple sight of brown,
a saving thread through solitude and drifts.
To find the way out of the wilderness,
I need only walk a little deeper into the woods.

COLUMBINE POETS OF COLORADO AWARD, Contest 23 (Any Month of the Year)

First Place, Jean Bell, Evergreen, CO

Sarcasm in December

Sarcastic, this white day
chuckles as I dance
an unexpected tango
across the icy porch.

He insists that windblown
is the most popular style
of the season, and I wear it
no matter what I want.

He mocks as I try to start the car:
"Ten degrees below zero and you
thought you'd slide by another winter
with this old clunker, didn't you?"

He chortles as I reprise the tango,
this time with a two-thousand-pound
vehicle as my dance partner.
Fortunately, I clear the turn.

But I will have the last laugh.
Smooth and powdery, I ski
the sparkling slope. I'll coax
some joy from Old Man Winter yet.

August

The world is on fire—the sun so hot
Here in the street on this Dog Day afternoon
Earth itself seems a sun,
The lung-searing air burning all around us
With a star's astronomical chemistry.

The heat! The heat! is the one thought
We can think in this weather,
The one-note song we whine
In pity for our wilting selves.

Cicadas sing again and again
In the white-hot radiance of the hour,
Their songs ripping the sky
Like the electric teeth of a saw.
Something in us pulls taut
Until it can stretch no more,
Until we feel our minds close to breaking.

Now we regret falling out of love
With winter and its cold winds,
With its storms of ice and snow,
And we wonder what madness
Ever made us tire of it.

COLUMBINE POETS OF COLORADO AWARD, CONTEST 23 (ANY MONTH OF THE YEAR)
Third Place, Diane Glancy, Gainesville, TX

March

March is a lion for all who know the wind.
March. March, he said, to war.
March is from the Middle French *marchier,* to trample,
probably of Germanic origin—
akin to Old High German *macron*, to mark.
First known use 15th century.
March is a boat with open sail.
March is a pick-pocket.
A corset blown off the clothes-line like a flying squirrel.
The waves of March are bark.
Bark has ridges of incoming waves.
I tell you this because I have seen the rough sea.
There is a certain grief to March.
You thought winter was over, but it returns.
March in made of broken parts.
March is cunning. It wears armor.
March is a roily sea.
March is a bowl held between the waves.
Otherwise I roll across the table and fall onto the floor.
I see the underside of tables and chairs.
I see the mark of the manufacturer.
The underside of March is stamped by God.
You are my bowl, Lord, a concave kingdom
in which to hold hibiscus bulbs or turnips.
March is a nest—as the sea nests on the land.
Birds fly in March. A nest is woven by a beak.
March never returns what it borrowed.
March finds solace in its broken parts—
is something blown but turned around with uprising.
March, he said, to war. March.

MORTON D. PROUTY & ELSIE S. PROUTY MEMORIAL AWARD, CONTEST 24 (NATURE POEM)

First Place, Stephen Curry, Jackson, MS

Nature's Law

1

Along a by-canal of marshy land,
The alligator stalks his feathery prey.
In motionless motion he seems to stand
In place to escape the city bird's survey.
Amid the knees of cypress trees he waits.
He has the time. His forebears were before
The dinosaurs not much unlike in traits.
The duck stands close now—not a foot from shore!

2

Then a thrashing of waters, much quicker than the eye!
A smoke of feathers like thistle down does fly!
But no longer the bird, now vised in a toothy maw,
The on-looking lilies have witnessed Nature's Law!

MORTON D. PROUTY & ELSIE S. PROUTY MEMORIAL AWARD, CONTEST 24 (NATURE POEM)
Second Place, Kathy Lohrum Cotton, Anna, IL

Amargosa, the Hide-and-Seek River

Like a desert Sherlock, I track secrets
of the Mojave's hide-and-seek river
as she stitches her long slender thread
in and out, above and beneath
moonscaped earth.

For 185 miles I trace Amargosa's spare signs
between her Pahute Mesa headwaters
and Death Valley demise,
finding above-ground clues at Beatty
and that no-clothes-required
warm-springs enterprise of Tecopa,
then catching the trace of her spine that
flash-floods to life in rare rainstorms.

But it's the river's riveting appearance
as Mojave's last remaining oasis
that takes my breath. In that wild
incongruity of wetlands and desert
she shows herself as a turquoise spring
whose bottom has never been reached,
as pools teeming with relic species
of ancient fish, a place for plants and
animals found nowhere else on earth.
Here, the secretive river rises
to surprise the desert with a kiss.

Stalactite/Stalagmite

How many blind centuries did you pass in the dark
clinging to Mother Earth's underbelly
pale grey as a possum joey
and timidly reach
pointy face
down
s
t
r
e
t
c
h
i
n
g
your
wet nose
bumping the ground
tongue tasting the limestone
before deciding it was safe enough
to build a stepstool and meet yourself halfway?

POETS' ROUNDTABLE OF ARKANSAS AWARD, CONTEST 25 (ANY SUBJECT)

First Place, Karen Kay Bailey, Blanchard, OK

The Neglected Gift

I peered inside the dusty chest—
Memories rushed like meadowlark
From each memento that had survived
The consequences of my unsettled life.

One, given only casual attention,
Was a gift from my grandmother.

I opened the tan, leatherette lid
And lifted eyeglasses from garnet velvet—
Noticing at once, intricate designs
Etched in the round gold-filled rims,
Nose bridge and thin temples.
The glossy, pink pearl nose pads
Deepened a sense of her elegance,
And a note inside the small flat case
Revealed her name, Lillian Hall.

I held the shining spectacles in my hands,
Carefully adjusted them to my face—
Then gazed through the polished glass.

I imagined her reading the daily news,
A novel, or poetry by a warm fire—
Removing them when she brushed her hair,
Lay down beside someone she loved,
Or when she wiped away her tears.

I sighed in awe of her presence—
To think a kindred spirit could evoke
Such deep affection through silent lens.

POETS' ROUNDTABLE OF ARKANSAS AWARD, Contest 25 (Any Subject)
Second Place, Mark Barton, Mechanicsburg, PA

Sighting Birdsong in the Pyrenées

By an old stone chapel, where a
bald escarpment oversees
great geometries of wildness,
birding in the Pyrenées
introduced us to new vultures,
and an owlet near the trees.

Sharp and lustrous then, a high note
cleansed our path below the butte
near a coruscating creek. The
afterimage left me mute:

Picture, if you will the sunlight
—that's how I'll describe the sound—
sunlight flashing on bright metal
from the verdure where we found
—piercing with its blinding whistles—
hidden low above the ground,

"Nightingale," our guide said softly.

Stridently, the unseen bird
thrust a throaty vision, and I
saw his song…as well as heard.

Yesterday

Oh, we rocked—
rocked to transistor radios
placed on
cinderblock/wood-plank bookcases,
carried on shoulders,
propped against trees—
while we rolled
in strawberry fields,
on back seats,
in recessed doorways,
on couches dumped
at charity collection stations.
California dreaming.
We wore flowers and beads,
took off our bras, our shirts,
rolled joints,
and rocked to grooooovy
unfocused
profound visions and colors,
all strobing to the vibration
of music blasting,
long beautiful hair
shining gleaming in
lava lamps revolving
in dark rooms,
neon face and body paint
glowing in black light.
We rocked and rolled
eight miles high,
born to be wild, born to be free,
all peace and love.

How can it be
our midnight hour.

LOUISIANA STATE POETRY SOCIETY AWARD, CONTEST 26 (ANY SUBJECT)

First Place, John W. Coppock, Tuttle, OK

from SYMPOSIUM—A Play: No. 1 and No. 2

1: *Women of the Chorus*

A thought is partial sense of statics fired
to fugue through fluted passages of nerves
with contents time impressed and nature wired
and sieved through consciousness to those reserves
that newer impulse stirs until inspired
to resonate with worded memories,
but still we say we will our histories
when data sorted over ganglia
rephrase an idiom that nature grooved
one time in software and in viscera.
Not will, but thought's eruptions have removed
old lusts, to harmonize that orchestra
which plays polyphonies in keys evolved
to timed environments the mind resolved.

2: *Men of the Chorus*

Among the residues of ancient times
are reasonings of minds now passed the flesh
that sensed reality in pantomimes
of pressures as we have but knew no mesh
of modern terms, nor miracles, nor climes
more centuries about a shifting pole
have oozed through consciousness to silt the soul
to slower currents of meditation.
Unique our moment; yet we hesitate
to change, from such long veneration
for human thoughts now parted from the state
that made them sensible, and no relation
have we to these except to what the genes
have grooved immutably into routines.

LOUISIANA STATE POETRY SOCIETY AWARD, CONTEST 26 (ANY SUBJECT)
Second Place, J. Paul Holcomb, Double Oak, TX

I Never Liked That Tie Anyway

> *Oh, I have been to Ludlow fair*
> *and left my necktie God knows where,*
> *And carried half way home, or near,*
> *Pints and quarts of Ludlow beer:....*
>
> ~ A.E. Housman, "A Shropshire Lad"

Oh, I have been to Ludlow fair
and played the oboe, second chair,
but when our music stopped I saw
a tomcat place its right front paw
upon the lead conductor's hair.
Oh, I have been to Ludlow fair

and left my necktie God knows where.
Under the lead conductor's glare
is where I left that cursed necktie
because the cat chose soon to try
my ascot in the maestro's hair
and left my necktie God knows where.

And carried half way home, or near—
the tabby made it very clear
the tie was his, my neck was free—
and I dry-mouthed a no-scratch plea,
confessed my feline-phobic fear,
and carried half way home, or, near

pints and quarts of Ludlow beer.
In my right eye, a single tear,
betrayed my dread of catty claws.
My bravery revealed sad flaws,
my recipe for staunching fear:
pints and quarts of Ludlow beer.

LOUISIANA STATE POETRY SOCIETY AWARD, Contest 26 (Any Subject)
Third Place, Christine H. Boldt, Temple, TX

The Place for Lost Children

America and I sat down together in the place for lost children.... ~Yevgeny Yevtushenko

A bench outside the zoo in Central Park
is where lost children wait for what may be.
The poet sits there with America,
as he tells us, in "New York Elegy,"

His words suggest both he and she are lost:
their goals are blurred, their purposes unclear.
I think of my country as she wonders how
to help the many and the one cohere.

Rules that we once lived by, now set aside,
our people swamped by violence and greed,
saying absolutes are meant for others,
that our lapses are justified by need.

Is there room for me on that tear-blurred bench?
I too feel rootless, unaffirmed, exiled,
because if America has lost her way,
then what am I but a nationless child?

First Place, Catherine Moran, Little Rock, AR

Crisis hot-line

Last night I held you by a slender wire
snaking across the wall of midnight.
It coiled around my fingers,
winding into the circuits of your voice.
We danced along that tightrope
in couple-colored,
sprung-rhythm balance.
I followed your lead with caution,
listening and pleading,
twisting words to deceive the moment.
Through it all that looming dread
kept shouting over
every choice you seemed to have,
until there was no other voice.

I heard you
sliding down the very line I held.
You were a single drop of plasma
spiraling in a code-blue oval,
stinging past my outstretched hands
like a razor drowning in space.
I stretched out far into that night
to stop the fall,
but only fear was crouching there
in dark silence.
With bone-taut fingers
I clasped that solitary cord
for hours and hours and hours.

FREEDA MURPHY MEMORIAL AWARD, Contest 27 (Any Subject)
Second Place, Fay Guinn, Jonesboro, AR

Too Much Bliss

I wanted a light, low-calorie lunch
so I could eat a four-course bunch
of fresh, Pacific Ocean fish at night.
I chose a sumptuous soup, culinary delight,
rose petal pink and just as smooth,
thick as an old-fashioned, strawberry
milkshake made by a soda fountain jerk,
mountain peak of whipped cream on top.
Taste buds smiled as it traveled
over rapacious tongue eagerly
awaiting the next mouthful mother lode
until bowl was left with streaks
and swirls of color, scraped by spoon
around the canvas of white, ceramic bowl.
Licking would be rude, so a crusty
piece of bread was used to sop
last remaining drop of liquid gold.
Oh the heavenly bliss of tomato bisque.
But then digestion, once a gentle stream
becomes a roiling river, angrily displeased
with butter, fat, and heavy cream.
Intestines groan from overload.
What seemed like gastronomical feast,
becomes a fleeting joy, twisting bowels
into a herd of wild, stampeding swine.
Too much bliss.

FREEDA MURPHY MEMORIAL AWARD, CONTEST 27 (ANY SUBJECT)

Third Place, Diane Glancy, Gainesville, TX

Card Stock

I open my hands and birds fly out.
My great-grandfather was a fugitive
when he settled in Arkansas.
He returns sometimes from the other world.
I hear him eat a carrot by my window.
The owls complain.
The only noise at night should be theirs.
I am prone to running myself.
I don't know what from.
The jetsam that washes up in weather?
Hay rolls graze in the fields.
The morning fog is a fugitive also.
My great-grandfather lost his land
when the Norfork River was dammed.
His fields underwater now.
The fish are the herds of his pasture.
The turtles. The frogs.
When a story is written it is paper.
When it is told it is card stock.
His base-camp now the moon—
tossed like a ball in a wide field.

CLAIRE VAN BREEMEN DOWNES MEMORIAL AWARD, Contest 28 (Sonnet)
First Place, Mary Tindall, Whitehouse, TX

Doll
Shakespearean Sonnet

Her needle turns a string of yarn from ball
to playful face to fill with cotton dreams.
A growing form is shaped by sewing small
and skillful stitches into even seams

which swaddle wishes tight enough to keep.
She takes her maker's gift, a teasing smile
and open, dreamy eyes too wide to sleep.
She's stuffed and dressed in blue with pleasing style.

A shelf of favorite stories offers space
for Doll to share amid the bears who sing
and dolls who blink and grin and mirror grace.
From string to charm, as real as anything,

with button eyes and smile of yarn, she looks
alive and wise beside the picture books.

Discovering pigs
Shakespearean Sonnet

My third-grade class stepped crisp as flakes of corn
onto that farm. We left all books behind.
I watched some rumpled cows that country morn,
then skipped the barn to see what I could find.
I saw a pen and clambered up the rails
discovering some pigs with dirty backs.
They weren't like those in countless fairy tales,
and everything I saw just twisted all the facts.
Not one of these seemed soft and cute and pink.
They pawed the ground while rooting crusty snouts.
The smell alone just made my stomach sink,
and disappointment slowly turned to doubts.
    I sadly backed away from childhood's sense
    to leave cartoons and Disney on that fence.

CLAIRE VAN BREEMEN DOWNES MEMORIAL AWARD, Contest 28 (Sonnet)

Third Place, Janet Watson, Wesley Chapel, FL

At a Fundraiser for Cancer Victims
Shakespearean Sonnet

An unfair war, the fearsome contest fought
by those who battle cancer every day.
To weakened hearts, we send one valiant thought—
We shall not let your illness have its way!
Our lighted votives ring the dark, wet track,
where athletes have heard cheers for skill or speed.
Now all is hushed, revering those who lack
the strength that once was theirs when they had need.
Within this wreath of flames we now shall give
memorials of love for victims gone
and honor courage of brave friends who live.
Through blowing rain, will candles burn till dawn?

They will. And we will walk, though drenched to bone.
Let victims know they do not walk alone.

UTAH STATE POETRY AWARD, CONTEST 29 (HERITAGE)

First Place, Wendy Visser, Cambridge, Ontario

Remnants

...carved toy horse, keepsake from her oldest
who almost saw his first full year,
croup or question mark—
cherished wooden traveler brought by family
when they emigrated from the land
that grows both hardy temperaments and tulips.

...tin box coffins two bullets,
the size of life, one per war,
two generations of fatherless sons—
badges of sacrifice
bequeathed to freedom and to male heir.

...moccasins and peace pipe
rolled in a buffalo robe—
fringe and feather legacy,
from a way back great great
on the red side of a maternal connection.

...gun, no longer loaded,
granny's gift from her log cabin life—
no explanation needed.

...a bottled Jack Daniels left behind
by the black sheep persona of gramps,
whose quip that no one's perfect,
fit him like his worn-well wool cardigan—
his souvenir peeks out
from under the flounce of my coverlet.

Skeletons bored with the closet
have changed location;
lay themselves under the bed,
their voices ride the back roads
to a place anchored tight
in the land of my heritage.

UTAH STATE POETRY AWARD, CONTEST 29 (HERITAGE)

Second Place, Lucille Morgan Wilson, Des Moines, IA

Tracks Through Winter

A relentless wind sculpts ever-changing swirls
over the path between house and barn. In January
fury, it scoops up loose handfuls to fling in our faces
as Dad and I make our way out for morning chores.

I shiver, yearn to be back under cozy covers,
but know Old Bess will be stomping in her stall,
impatient for us to come for the rich, warm milk
she'll yield to Dad's strokes, while I carry a pail of oats
to the horses in the other side of the barn.
The calico cat rouses from the haymow to claim
her portion of milk. Some will flow over bowls
of steaming oatmeal; some will fill little sister's cup.

At almost eight, I'm proud to be Dad's helper. I struggle
to keep pace, head down to blunt the driving snow,
and jump from one overshoe pit to the next big white hole,
landmarks that will be erased long before we make our way
back to the house. "C'mon, Son…almost there." His voice
blows back to me. Saving breath, watching for
the next footprint, I don't reply. Decades later,
trying to discern the next step amid drifts
of indecision, bucking storms that obscure the path,
a kindly breeze wafts his voice to me. I see
the prints of honesty, hard work and tolerance
still clear and deep—just one step ahead.

I hope he hears my answer.

Family of Six Portrait, 1918

Rushing past the portrait on the doily-covered table
to greet the crush of mourners with nods and nods,
she supposes she should face it down or shroud
that image too, along with the blacked-out mirrors.

In that 1916's sepia she sits squarely fixed, finely dressed,
proud beside her husband, flanked by oldest daughter and son,
the younger two cross-legged on the photographer's rug—
complete family of six, framed and displayed, today
disarrayed; husband felled by Spanish flu's deadly reach.

Surrounded by relatives looking weepy, she seeks
him out, then remembers he's gone.
She eyes them sadly, knowing beyond hugs and sighs
they'll provide no relief, though possibly a meal
grown cold in transit.

No time to grieve the irretrievable.
A baby boy still milking from her breast
and the two young ones tugging at her skirt
while the old ones bear platters and pass
glances at each other, refraining from tears and talk.

The old uncle coughs. The baby wakes and wails.
Removed from the crowd, she sits and rocks
as he nurses greedily beneath her black shawl.

When will they all be gone? Will any food be left?
The young daughter puts her head upon one knee,
and not outdone, the newly crippled young son,
polio survivor, claims the other.

Anchored to chair, yet unmoored, she shuts
her eyes, she bites a nail, tastes cemetery dirt—
and *Feh*, she spits; the children start; she stands,
baby under arm, and marches to the crowd,
shooing them out the door. Go! Go! Time to leave.
Five lives to feed. Widowed now, no time to grieve.

CSPS JAMES E. MacWHINNEY MEMORIAL AWARD, Contest 30 (Blank Verse)

First Place, Barbara J. Funke, St. George, UT

The Invention of Nouns

All-purpose in your lexicon are *that*
and *those*, real names of things ignored, replaced
by sweeping gestures, fingers pointed *there*.
I'm using that, so I lay down the spoon
and you pick up the knife I've left alone.
The spoon remains unused by both of us.

Communication's off the rails again.
It (your vocabulary's mystery)
might drive me to the brink of violence.

Now, like a surgeon mumbling, *Scalpel; sponge*,
you indicate the dishcloth, hand held out.
And when that orphan noun drips from your mouth
without a context, I dry off the spoon,
relieved it hasn't any kind of point
in this exchange and grateful that you choose
to place clean out of sight the knife you've used.

Your patience drained when I fail to respond,
you gripe, *We never can communicate.*
We used to end each other's sentences!

Correct me if I'm wrong—I'm sure you will—
but I think that was long before you ceased
to show appreciation for the noun,
specific name for what you have in mind,
so I might get a hint which track your train
of thought is certain that it's traveling on.

CSPS JAMES E. MacWHINNEY MEMORIAL AWARD, CONTEST 30 (BLANK VERSE)

Second Place, Alison Chisholm, Birkdale, U.K.

Double Exposure

Nobody knows for sure how he found out
the secret we'd protected for so long,
but now our very lives are put at risk
each time the book is read, the film is screened.
He guessed the access route: who would believe
a tale of tumbling through rabbit holes
that plunged so far?   And yet he knows that growth
and shrinking are controlled by *Eat Me, Drink Me*.
He knew the rules of Caucus Races, knew
the key's location and the Rabbit's fan.

He lived the nightmare all of us have dreamed,
becoming giants in our wonderland,
and filling houses, room by room, until
our limbs burst from the doors and windows. He
had met the caterpillar, taken tea
with Dormouse, Hare and Hatter, seen the Duchess.
How else could he conceive the Cheshire cat,
pig-baby, the flamingo croquet mallets?

However he found out about our land,
a simple etiquette should have restrained.
He should have kept his writing for those tomes
of mathematics. Secrets of our lives
could have remained an earth-deep mystery.

Now we are forced to play the hand he dealt,
conduct our lives aware we've been exposed,
and any time another human may
break through the barrier between our worlds
and blindly blunder into our domain.

One thing we hope: those other characters
who live like us in worlds just parallel
to his, but in their own reality,
still keep their undiscovered status, still
live out their chessboard lives in innocence,
where interfering authors and the girls
of their imagination cannot reach.

Aftermath

But it is the doing of old things, small acts that are just and right; And the doing of them over and over again.
~Ella Wheeler Wilcox

Light drizzles beyond partly open blinds
onto the window ledge of my mom's
hospital room; some handmade get-well cards
are displayed like art on a museum wall.
Mother can't read them; there's more moon than sun
in her eyes. We read the cards to her, slice
her meat, scoop her vegetables, sweeten
her coffee for weeks after the stroke. I tap
the yellow limb of a pencil against
the spine of Diane Frank's *Canon for Bears
and Ponderosa Pines*. My sister sits
on the edge of the bed. We watch Mama
hold a plastic fork with an unsteady
tilt of hand. When rice falls from the prongs, we
do not disturb the sticky grains beached like
white sand on her hospital gown. We take
deep grateful breaths as autumn's red fiery
leaves burn cooling days off the calendar.

ILLINOIS STATE POETRY SOCIETY AWARD, CONTEST 31 (BOOKS)
First Place, Caroline Johnson, Willow Springs, IL

On Listening to Middle Eastern Poetry at the Poetry Foundation in Chicago

An Iraqi poet speaks about a trapped bird
as I peer outside glass at a busy Chicago street.
Around me the city breathes. Pedestrians
strut like pigeons, hurry in two directions.
A parking attendant in an orange vest
practices capitalism, collects money.

> *The bilingual poet chants, "O Iraq," sings*
> *to his wife, Hadbaa, in his native tongue*
> *the language of love and lovers.*

Yellow and white taxis race each other.
Trees lean into the Chicago wind.
Shoppers carry bags: *Whole Foods,*
Macy's, Carson's. A jogger whizzes by.

> *A Syrian refugee tells of fleeing Turkey*
> *and sailing to Lesbos, where the poet*
> *Sappho spoke and wrote of Love.*

Run, jogger, run. Run to the light
while poets wearing white speak
about the blind, and it is April 23,
Shakespeare's day of birth and death.

> *The poet says he spent time in a refugee*
> *camp, a number pinned to his chest.*
> *Neither Odysseus nor Aeneas, he has*
> *no home in exile, but he escaped death.*

The cries of poets are bullets to my blood.
Thousands of poetry books stand imprisoned
behind glass. I swallow and watch as dreams
disappear in the kiln of desire.

> *Shall I compare thee to a summer's day?*
> *...Rough winds do shake the darling buds of May,*
> *And summer's lease hath all too short a date.**

*Lines from William Shakespeare's "Sonnet 18"

ILLINOIS STATE POETRY SOCIETY AWARD, Contest 31 (Books)
Second Place, Kathy Lohrum Cotton, Anna, IL

Two Views of the Plaza

May 1935
He's a proud young Berliner, a university student
cheered on by crowds as large as a city,
lining the triumphant torch-lit parade route

to the Opera Plaza. Some 20,000 books,
piled high in waiting trucks, are passed
hand to hand toward a massive log pyre,

and he is the first to toss black-listed
volumes into the flames—the paper roar
rising along with passionate speech and song.

April 1995
On Yom HaShoah, a student from Tel Aviv
visits the plaza, kneels on the stones at a thick
glass square, set flush into this pavement where

once crowds applauded as banned pages fueled
an infamous book-burning. He stares down into
the bare white shelves of a sunken memorial,

Berlin's blank library for 20,000 ghosted tomes.
Century-old words on a plaque sting his eyes—
the bronzed quote of a banned Jewish poet:

> *That was only a prelude,*
> *there where they burn books,*
> *they burn in the end people.*
>   –Heinrich Heine, 1820

ILLINOIS STATE POETRY SOCIETY AWARD, CONTEST 31 (BOOKS)

Third Place, Crystie Cook, Sandy, UT

Booksmarts

"You'll never spy on me again!"
the sinister villain bellowed.
"I'll come back in a month and see
if starving has left you mellowed!"
The man's laugh echoed evilly;
the wooden door slammed like thunder.
Then Nancy Drew, there in the dark,
was left to reflect and wonder.
"Oh, my," mused Nancy ruefully.
"Well, no one can call me clueless,
although this villain's left me here,
locked up in chains and shoeless."

Just then a swell idea came;
she rubbed her head against the wall
until she heard a pinging sound—
a hairpin had worked loose to fall.
Now Nancy leaned on down to pick
the hairpin up between her lips
and started to pick at the lock
while thinking of more clever quips.
An hour passed by, but doggedly
she worked the lock, until it clicked
and fell to clatter on the ground.
"Ah ha!" cried Nancy. "I'm not licked!"

She wriggled loose from all the chains
and used a crowbar on the door.
"How lucky I have lost my shoes;
I'll make no noise upon the floor!"
So Nancy sneaked out of the house
and went to call local police.
How soon the villain stood, handcuffed,
accused by all of those he'd fleeced!
He glared at Nancy, who was cool
and countered, "Hmm, you'll never win.
Too bad you never learned to read,
or you'd have known about that pin!"

OHIO AWARD, Contest 32 (Any Subject)

First Place, Joshua Conklin, Amherst, NH

Ode to the Cochlea

Snagging tympanic vibrations
you shape the sound,
wrap it in mollusk membranes.

Cilia sway,
hum along with trumpet solos,
bang heads to hip hop beats,
tap staccato on nerve endings.

Electrons, boiled into the brain stem,
explode
red hot and neural
into gray matter.

You make frequency beauty,
decipher decibels,
and codify rhythmic runes.

What worthy praise can we offer
for your semicircular canals
that spin fluid,
dizzy us,
like some fantastic lover?

OHIO AWARD, CONTEST 32 (ANY SUBJECT)

Second Place, Kathy Lohrum Cotton, Anna, IL

Lightning Rod
for the activist

Your upright head,
arrow of your straight spine
as you stand

staunch like redwood,
like mountain ash
ledge-high,

daring lightning
to kiss the copper rod
of your soaring words,

to blaze down your bones,
ground its voltage
through your deep roots.

When the thunderhead
rolls in, steals light
from every window,

I hear you
shouting against the storm,
the spitting sky.

You lift your arms,
take fire
for all of us.

OHIO AWARD, CONTEST 32 (ANY SUBJECT)
Third Place, Markay Brown, St. George, UT

Undressing Billy Collins

*after his poem, "Taking off Emily
Dickinson's Clothes"*

The whole idea is too brash.
After all, he seems quite shy
when he's not at the lectern.
How to approach him, broach the subject
of what lies beneath his rumpled suit,
narrow lapels, hip skinny tie—fashion
he probably picked up from his students.

To make him comfortable
I say, *Just imagine you're
in that bathhouse in Istanbul.*

I quote from his foray into
Miss Dickinson's corset.
He loosens his burgundy tie.
I help him out of his jacket,
unbutton his button-down collar.
He speaks in the voice of the dog
he put to sleep, the one that wrote
a poem of all the ways he disliked
Billy, of all people.

Then he changes the subject to nine horses
far from the pasture and a cube of sugar.

My ex-laureate lingers over what seems
aimless, but then a secret surfaces
nearly plain as the glasses on his face
now pushed up on his balding head.

He reaches down and unties his Italian
leather shoes, removes his argyle socks,
then Billy sails around the room
in plaid boxers.
Who could ask for more?

First Place, Richard Hurzeler, Tyler, TX

Where Worlds Collide

Sam slams into my waiting chest
Autistic zest
For him it's fun
To hit and run

At times he spins around and round
In circles bound
His inner world
Where he's unfurled

I, Papa, keeping him in prayer
He eyes me there
I sit on rug
And wait for hug

MINUTE AWARD, CONTEST 33 (A MINUTE POEM)
Second Place, Jerri Hardesty, Brierfield, AL

Random Act

The children play on slides and swings
as parent brings
a picnic lunch
to feed the bunch.

A woman sits alone nearby.
They wonder why.
They offer chips
and veggie dips.

Her eyes well up with grateful tears,
"Oh, thank you dears,
I'll gladly eat
this special treat."

MINUTE AWARD, CONTEST 33 (A MINUTE POEM)

Third Place, V. Kimball Barney, Kaysville, UT

Wishful Fishing

At times I walk along the stream
and often dream
of all the fish
that on my dish
could cause my mouth to salivate,
or on my plate
could make me smile,
but all the while
I know I'd have to fish, you see,
and that won't be,
because I know
I'll never go.

POETRY SOCIETY OF MICHIGAN AWARD, CONTEST 34 (FREE VERSE)
First Place, Micki Blenkush, St. Cloud, MN

This Year's Garden

The name of this ceremony is patience.
My husband is threading apart
salvaged tightgrown kohlrabi and broccoli
from his coworker's greenhouse.

Hours crouched and kneeling,
filling in our barren patches
with plants acclimated to clinging in a tangle,
now weak and wilted when separated.

Everything he finds has someplace to be.
Cans and plastic bottles gathered
on his way home from work
pack our recycling bin each week.

River-worn driftwood carried
branch by branch fashions
his workshop centerpiece,
an indoor tree.

Near our first garden, he planted
strawberries in the shade of pines.
I knew it was a waste of time
and said so before and after.

Today I watch from inside how he tends
what he has to know may die.
Rather than simply spray the hose,
he carries a leaking can, his tender rain.

POETRY SOCIETY OF MICHIGAN AWARD, Contest 34 (Free Verse)

Second Place, Dave Harvey, Talent, OR

A Sign, a Jingle

In a tiny campground,
I pack panniers in gray light.
In thin fog, I push my bike out to pavement,
swing aboard, and resume the uphill grind
I ground for hours yesterday.

I reach the summit,
begin to coast toward the next river;
air is cool, swift around my body.
I ride out from under a smear of cloud
and cast a shadow
as the sun clears the ridge that is
my eastern horizon.

Something hangs in air,
twenty feet away,
above and ahead of me:
a bird, gliding, occasional wing flaps,
pacing me as I hum down
the two-lane: a gull?
No! A crow!

His head turns from side to side
as he looks back, keeps me in view.
He keeps pace with me, holding station.
Mostly he glides, but when he flaps
to maintain speed,
the rising sun glints gold
on his wings' undersides.
For a breathless minute, maybe two,
he stays above me, guides me around a curve,
around another, then lifts and flies off.

Did God the Father/Mother think it'd be fun
to jingle my keys this way?
Or was this my native spirit guide, Crow Brother,
come to join me in rejoicing
at the goodness of this day?

Yes.

POETRY SOCIETY OF MICHIGAN AWARD, Contest 34 (Free Verse)
Third Place, Robert Schinzel, Highland Village, TX

A Long View Through Time

The sun explodes
across the eastern escarpments
near Glen Canyon Dam,
Lake Powell itself illuminated
in kaleidoscopic glitter
reflected from surface ripples.
The lake stretches like a centipede
across landscapes of stone,
scarred and stained shorelines
in sharp contrast to water's azure tones.

The marks of damage and concrete features
hint at some failure of mankind
that mocks the natural balance,
an ephemeral sty in eon's eye.
How soon sediment will fill the reservoir,
the dam crack and tumble away,
liberate a river in its flow to the sea,
cutting, carving, shaping the chasm
for a few more million years.

The scene across this high plateau country
through reservations, pueblo ruins,
canyon lands, transports me
to a kind of nether time, a cerebral state
trapped between sleep and awake,
dream and conscious thought,
each view turned to gold
by a visual Midas touch. I see my fate,
like that of the land, as a journey in stone,
rough edges weathering with time,
transforming canyons and mesas
to tranquil peneplain.

MISSISSIPPI POETRY SOCIETY AWARD, Contest 35 (Sonnet)

First Place, Budd Powell Mahan, Dallas, TX

The Vietnam Memorial
Shakespearean Sonnet

The juried choice was Maya Lin's design
as stark and black as war or clotted blood
of heroes. But soon critics drew a line,
attacked the choice and flung a wave of mud,
an ugly blitz on Lin and her dark walls.
The jurors held their ground with dignity,
stood firm, resolved to shout down nasty calls
deriding age and sex, ethnicity.
Misogyny and bias did not win,
long granite walls were quarried, set in place.
The human name etched in the shiny skin,
became a site of pilgrimage and grace.
The controversy now is little known
by those who finger-trace the chiseled stone.

MISSISSIPPI POETRY SOCIETY AWARD, Contest 35 (Sonnet)

Second Place, Dave Harvey, Talent, OR

Deadly Birds
Cuban Missile Crisis, 1962

Caribbean Sonnet

Of those fall days, a few things still come back:
The nightmare message stopping us before we ate,
Three words on pale-green flimsy, cold as fate:
SET DEFCON TWO—just leave! No time to pack!
Now get your ships to sea! Don't wonder why!
Before tomorrow dawn, the birds could fly!

Back even then in nineteen-sixty-two,
Both sides had deadly birds, nuclear-tipped;
Each time the diplomats got in a stew,
The missile pukes into their silos slipped,
And, standing by, they'd hold their hearts and wait
To send mass death to those they did not hate.

So out we steamed to where the waves rolled high,
We hoped no deadly birds came to our sky.

To the Former Child: Directions for Your Day
Kyrielle Sonnet

Play chase with butterflies and find
you left the world you knew behind;
you wandered, dreaming, right into
a road that bends beyond your view.

Play hide and seek among the trees
then catch a dandelion breeze
and launch a tuft of wish off to
a road that bends beyond your view.

Skip rocks across a springtime stream.
(The water's colder than it seemed.)
Then count some daisies—*pick a few!*—
on roads that bend beyond your view.

Play chase with butterflies and find
a road that bends beyond your view.

JESSE STUART MEMORIAL AWARD, CONTEST 36 (ANY SUBJECT)

First Place, Maurine Haltiner, Salt Lake City, UT

Nosing About the Stars

On black nights I wonder
if space stinks. My eyes spot
a zoo of stars arranged in old patterns:
goaty *Capricorn*, its wattle
of stray dwarfs spinning
down-neck—a faint crab & raging
bull—dipping bears, paws poised to snatch
Pisces from the sky—*Draco*
Dragon—*Leo Lion*—& a unicorn
dying to meet a virgin. When their jaws open

(in unison) for a bite of dark matter, when
they yowl & growl in the night, surely
cosmic odor insults all the gods, demi-gods, &
hemi-demi gods nosing
about—even ancients divorced
from mortal concern, unless

there's no star scent at all—a vacuum
of smell—no whiffs from riff-raff in the zoo,
no blazing suns' swirling smoke, no puffs
from red giants snuffed
by twists of time, not a hint of sulfur
from a single boiling comet born beyond
the *Arm of Orion*. I'd hoped for a devilish perfume
(*My Sin*, at least). Might inner &
outer space (really) be fragrance blind? I believe it

to be possible, until *Sirius* & *Procyon*,
first magnitude canines down a dipper of dark energy
(slightly scorched, faintly metallic) & bark
(once only), astonishing
this old dog
cold-shouldering the moon.

Graft: Kisses and Roses

Grandpa had been dead twenty years or more
when her neighbor started to flirt with Grandma.
Anyway, that's what I told her, half-teasing.
Oh, no, Susan, he's just a nice man next door.
I was in my own wild-oat days, or at least
as much as any shy college freshman can be.
Henry had moved in, a bachelor of fifty
and still blond, tall, blue-eyed.
I wormed the story out of her reticence…
It seems when Grandma was spending all spring
babying her nasturtiums, marigolds, and zinnias,
he had taken up the thread of gardening and
offered to teach her how to graft roses.
Her one old non-named bush was aging and
plagued with mildew—she fretted silently over it.
Blushing, she told me they'd walked to the city
park six blocks away, and (*No one was watching,
Susan*) with shears from an inner jacket pocket,
he snipped parts of the roses she most admired:
the lovely pink Peace, Mr. Lincoln for its perfume.
What would they say about my stealing roses?
They bent together trimming and tying.
Did he try to kiss or hold hands? *What a thing
to say, Susan!* My own darkling explorations
of the body's demands—Jack's mouth and later
Brian's and the dark of cars— made me suspect
her protestations. After all, my grandparents
were permanently reserved, but they'd had
three children. Well, the mysteries of couples
and the barriers of modesty—or was
it caginess? The roses thrived. When she showed
them to me the next spring, proud but not
confessing their origin, not saying park, neighbor,
trespass, by then I had already been gathering
my own roses.

JESSE STUART MEMORIAL AWARD, Contest 36 (Any Subject)
Third Place, Judith Feenstra, Maple Lake, MN

Stray Cat Traveling

While speeding on
a country road
in my vintage red Triumph
radio blasting
hair flying
pavement whizzing by
at seventy-five miles an hour
I glance across the ditch
and see a black cat
spring from a fence post
arch perfect in the air
plunge into the grass
then disappear…
      I mean man—
      that cat was traveling.

HUMOROUS POETRY AWARD, Contest 37 (Humorous, Rhymed)

First Place, Curt Vevang, Palatine, IL

The Grandpa Card

Grandpa worked for years in factories and mills,
    toiling and saving and paying the bills.
Then once he retired he was at a loss,
    because he found out he had a new boss.
It's really a shock at this time of life
    reporting daily to your loving wife.
But he's found a ruse to use to this end.
    It's the Grandpa Card which helps him contend.
If chores need doing, he can use this card,
    to take a long nap and ignore the yard.
When watching football, he can simply play
    his new Grandpa Card and food comes his way.
Politics or church, discuss a hot book,
    the Grandpa Card's played and he's off the hook.
No, not for Grandma, this card only suits
    "helpless" grandfathers and other old coots.

HUMOROUS POETRY AWARD, Contest 37 (Humorous, Rhymed)

Second Place, Sarah Morin, Fishers, IN

Checklist for the Picnic

We've packed the bug spray and sunscreen,
a camera to preserve the scene,
a tablecloth and two trash bags,
an old hammock that kind of sags,
paper plates, plastic utensils,
coloring books, crayons and pencils,
candles that smell of citronella,
in case of rain—that big umbrella,
sunglasses, your plastic visor,
napkins and hand sanitizer,
my broad-brimmed hat, and if we're able
let's squeeze in the new card table,
folding chairs with holders for drinks—
everything but the kitchen sink.
Now on the road, I hate to ask it:
did we put food in the basket?

HUMOROUS POETRY AWARD, Contest 37 (Humorous, Rhymed)
Third Place, Lorraine Jeffery, Orem, UT

New Bird Feeder

It hung brand new and graced the tree,
was filled with more than it could hold.
Neighborhood birds could eat for free,
help tiny sparrows brave the cold.

We watched them through the winter freeze,
but then came spring, and what a bummer.
They ate our berries, beans and peas,
we cussed them all that spring and summer.

BARBARA STEVENS MEMORIAL AWARD, Contest 38 (Any Serious Theme)
First Place, Budd Powell Mahan, Dallas, TX

Smoke
for my sister

She became smoke, a blue mist
coiling up to the last hour before dawn.
Her lungs stilled in the cavity
where they had cured and blackened
in a half century of
cigarette haze.

Now, she hovers by mall doors,
in fingers held from passing cars,
memory rising in the scent
of smolder.

BARBARA STEVENS MEMORIAL AWARD, Contest 38 (Any Serious Theme)
Second Place, Trina Lee, Oklahoma City, OK

Somewhere

Between love and loss
is a safe place…

It's quiet there…
a gentle breeze of hope
soft on my skin, not even
enough to ruffle my hair…
The only sounds are distant
with no melody…
It's almost light, but still not…

and I can breathe.

BARBARA STEVENS MEMORIAL AWARD, Contest 38 (Any Serious Theme)

Third Place, Larry Schulte, Albuquerque, NM

Home

The hawks circle slowly. Silently.
Paired solitude.

The carpet-bagging cranes
invade the silent space every year.

A few weeks in the spring,
a few in the autumn, migrating north or south.

The hawks remain,
weathering blizzard and summer sun.
Content in one place.

ALICE MACKENZIE SWAIM MEMORIAL AWARD, Contest 39 (Sonnet)

First Place, Budd Powell Mahan, Dallas, TX

Blood on the Mountains
Shakespearean Sonnet

Sangre de Cristo sunset draws a line,
a red stigmata on its rocky peaks.
The first to see it took it as a sign
of deity, the comfort each soul seeks.
The light could awe the simple to their knees,
and call the spirit to a flagging creed.
Now scientists list ice and snow, say these
reflect last light to make the mountains bleed.
They speak of aerosols, back-scattered glow
from particles suspended in the sky,
and smile at simple lore because they know
their truths are just too lucid to deny.

Yet, still believers seek the sunset's wraith
whose crimson alpenglow renews their faith.

ALICE MACKENZIE SWAIM MEMORIAL AWARD, Contest 39 (Sonnet)
Second Place, Joyce Shiver, Crystal River, FL

Cicada Summer
Shakespearean Sonnet

The roses bloomed more brilliantly, it seemed;
wild phlox and buttercups were everywhere,
and redbirds sang while Mother Nature beamed.
We wandered through the days without a care.
Cicadas hummed all day beneath the trees
the Sunday that we spent at City Park.
Bright butterflies cavorted in the breeze,
then fireflies rivaled stars in early dark.
It might have rained that summer, just a mist,
but I remember picnics in the sun
and lolling on the beach where first we kissed.
We sang our songs and danced till day was done.
Our joys were many and the troubles few
that wondrous summer when our love was new.

ALICE MACKENZIE SWAIM MEMORIAL AWARD, Contest 39 (Sonnet)

Third Place, J. Paul Holcomb, Double Oak, TX

Changing Seasons, Changing Colors
Terza Rima Sonnet

When Texas summer warmth begins to sear
the rose that bloomed in early April's spring,
the grower knows the time has come to fear
the heat and gives her fragile lawn the thing
it needs, a wet and cooling gentle shield.
She asks her hardy summer growth to bring
both cover for the early plants that yield
sweet spring-time blooms, plus August color, hues
that say, "I'm here to complement the field
with gold, off-white but not faint pinks or blues,
the muted tints that hint of gentle days—
before demanding autumn's russet, puce."
Wise growers know the seasons and their ways
and understand that pink, it never stays.

POETRY SOCIETY OF OKLAHOMA AWARD, Contest 40 (Trimeric)

First Place, Barbara Blanks, Garland, TX

Like His Ancestors

The words rolled like music from his tongue,
flowed down, surrounded her
with their heat and substance.
The way he danced—

flowed down, surrounded her—
mesmerized her. He conjured the grace
of a cougar, his eyes seeing an earlier time.

With their heat and substance,
his song and movements wept for his people,
who suffered and died along the Trail of Tears.

The way he danced
bent silver moonlight, reflecting his ancestors
in the liquid mirror of the pond.

POETRY SOCIETY OF OKLAHOMA AWARD, Contest 40 (Trimeric)

Second Place, Joshua Conklin, Amherst, NH

Questioning

Fatherhood doesn't come with an answer key,
once you understand your children, they change,
challenge everything.
You begin again, more tired than the day before.

Once you understand your children, they change,
testing your resolve.
Little revolutionaries who

challenge everything!
They provoke and negotiate,
probing for soft spots from dawn till dusk.

You begin again, more tired than the day before
but when they take your hand, seeking assurance, in an ever changing world,
you realize you have all the answers needed.

POETRY SOCIETY OF OKLAHOMA AWARD, Contest 40 (Trimeric)

Third Place, Dena R. Gorrell, Edmond, OK

Sometimes All That Glitters Isn't Gold

They are called the golden years…
sometimes I wonder why.
Gold hair turns to silver
and gravity makes us sag.

Sometimes I wonder why
newspaper print gets smaller
and it's harder to get things done.

Gold hair turns to silver
or falls out and makes us bald.
We have more ills, take more pills,

and gravity makes us sag.
It *does* take a lot of "gold" in the bank
to pay all our medical bills….

SAVE OUR EARTH AWARD, CONTEST 41 (ENVIRONMENTAL ISSUES)

First Place, Christina M. Flaugher, Mapleton, MN

Letter to the Daughter I Didn't Have

It isn't that I didn't want you.
I did.
In imagination I have cuddled you close
a million times.
I have tended your hurts, giggled with you.

But the world is bigger than my wants.
The planet groans
under the weight
of the parasite of humanity.

We ravage its surface
use up,
take and take.
We never give back.

You, my child whom I never created,
will never take without thought,
will never consume indiscriminately.
The sacrifice of you
is one drop
that tries to water the entire forest
before there are no more seeds to plant.

When your father and I leave this world
our legacy
will be the years we would
have given you.
Instead we saved them for the planet.

Try to understand,
that your unmaking
was not for lack of love,
but for something bigger than the desire
of two people,
and a third,
who will never hasten the destruction.

SAVE OUR EARTH AWARD, CONTEST 41 (ENVIRONMENTAL ISSUES)
Second Place, Amy Irish, Lakewood, CO

The Children of the Earth

They could be your sisters—
These seeds twirling in spring,
These bright and sacred Sufis of the air.

Wise as Buddhas. They laugh
At the glorious release,
Shouting into the open sky
As I throw them by fistfuls into flight.

They revel, then return.
To sprout and grow and thrive—
And die. Part of me

At every step. This is the nature
Of mothers, our two-sided gift.
This is the nature of life.
My other children do not curse this,

Deny this, destroy this.
They find joy in the cycles, the circles
We dance together. They live.

They could be your sisters—
Their future, an open hand.
When did you put a stop to dancing?
When did you close your fist so tight?

From the Voice of Water

We have tried to tell you, but our murmur
is muffled by the gurgle of wants
sung from your unquenchable throats.

When I say *we*, I mean drops of us
bound by viscous capacity to encompass
all that seeps, fills, or falls.

We thought you would have seen
lakes and streams turned to murk
or felt the littered burden

bobbing in our bellied oceans. A churn
of plastic bottles and bags.
Of doll parts, whiffle balls, and toy guns.

Meanwhile, compounded chemicals
camouflaged transparent in glasses poured
from your kitchen faucets. BPA, PFOA, PFOS—

alphabet soups residual from factories
and nonstick coatings and everything ever made
including medicines you take

swallowed and excreted. We are together
in a closed loop. Chlorinated
to pass the threshold measures.

You know how when you wake, thirsty
after illness, longing
only for the quench of water?

That is an echo. Your body
remembering its source, arcing like waves
toward home.

MASSACHUSETTS STATE POETRY SOCIETY AWARD, Contest 42 (Any Subject)

First Place, Beth Staas, Oak Brook, IL

Spring Demon

He doesn't care that a hexagon has six sides
or that *equation* means *equal*.
So he sits and picks at his cuticle
until it bleeds
then kicks off his right shoe
hitting Briana's desk with a klunk.

Mr. Bates sends him to the nurse
but a detour takes him outside,
each step a diaphanous leap
in a blue-jeaned ballet.
He makes faces through the window,
then loops and swoops in Dervish bliss
weaving his frenzied ecstasy.

We watch in bemused wonderment
then turn to wiser tasks.
The sun will set, the wind will blow
and evening's chill will send him home.

But until the stars come out
and the moon hangs low,
he'll ravish the sun and dance.

MASSACHUSETTS STATE POETRY SOCIETY AWARD, Contest 42 (Any Subject)

Second Place, Christine H. Boldt, Temple, TX

Middle School Choir Concert

The conductor's hands sketch arabesques.
The children purl as doves in cotes.
The conductor's hands, now butterflies,
are puddling over liquid notes.

"Stay the course, light a star,
Change the world wher'er you are."*

The pianist's hands above the keys
are doubled in the cabinet's oak.
Children chant of change and duty,
of noble yearning, simple folk.

"Stay the course, light a star,
Change the world wher'er you are."

The children's lips form rounded O's.
The boys, intense, are mouthing runes.
Bow-tied youth who hit high notes last year
are pimpled now, and growl their tunes.

"Stay the course, light a star,
Change the world wher'er you are."

The girls appear as waifs or matrons,
Spot-lit in their bunched-up dresses,
Each gown a slightly different hue.
Alice bands tame lengthy tresses.

"Stay the course, light a star,
Change the world wher'er you are."

The conductor's hands are lowered now,
But the children's last notes echo long.
The drilled efficiency with which they
Leave the risers is, itself, a song.

*Song lyric by Richard Le Gallienne

MASSACHUSETTS STATE POETRY SOCIETY AWARD, Contest 42 (Any Subject)
Third Place, Pat Underwood, Colfax, IA

Colostomy

You hide the bright pink protrusion
like a secret under your shirt,

snapped over like Tupperware.
Even when you slumber

it sleep talks under bed sheets,
stimulates nightmares

until you think of the rupture
with each passing hour.

This is a nervous morning,
the doctor's needle sterile

in the stainless steel drum.
You will awaken

to recovery room silence,
the words *stoma, ostomy, wafer,*

dissolving like stitches,
only threads of the haunting past.

POETRY SOCIETY OF TENNESSEE AWARD, Contest 43 (Pantoum)

First Place, Alison Chisholm, Birkdale, U.K.

One Moment in Time

Sun scorched the cobbles in the square,
and, temped by seductive heat,
we stopped our car to taste the air,
explore the plaza, church and street.

And tempted by seductive heat
we strolled together hand in hand,
explored the plaza, church and street,
the brittle grass and arid land.

We strolled together. Hand in hand
we found a bar and ordered wine.
The brittle grass and arid land
reached out to meet horizon's line.

We found a bar and ordered wine.
One tiny moment fixed; and we
reached out to meet horizon's line.
That second was infinity.

One tiny moment fixed, and we—
we stopped our car to taste the air.
That second was infinity.
Sun scorched the cobbles in the square.

POETRY SOCIETY OF TENNESSEE AWARD, CONTEST 43 (PANTOUM)

Second Place, Brenda Brown Finnegan, Ocean Springs, MS

A Different Thanksgiving

We celebrate, again, Thanksgiving Day
With friends and family gathered by our side.
Yet, this one, for us, is different in the way
We set the table, roast the turkey, bake the pies.

With friends and family gathered by our side
We share a meal in someone else's home.
They set the table, roast the turkey, bake the pies.
For nothing's left of what was once our own.

We share a meal in someone else's home;
Our china's a mosaic in the sand.
For nothing's left of what was once our own.
Katrina savaged our beloved homeland.

Our china's a mosaic in the sand.
With crystal shards shining in debris,
Katrina savaged our beloved homeland.
No house, no table, chairs, no normalcy.

With crystal shards shining in debris,
We gladly accept their hospitality.
No house, no table, chairs, no normalcy;
We join their hands with great humility.

We gladly accept their hospitality.
Yes, this one, for us, is different in the way
We join their hands with great humility.
And celebrate, again, Thanksgiving Day.

POETRY SOCIETY OF TENNESSEE AWARD, CONTEST 43 (PANTOUM)

Third Place, LaVern Spencer McCarthy, Blair, OK

He Loves Me Still...

He sends me roses for our special day.
They grow from vines he planted long ago.
Although he closed his eyes and slipped away,
he loves me still and always lets me know.

They grow from vines he planted long ago,
a balm against my sorrows in the night.
He loves me still and always lets me know
he watches from above where all is bright.

A balm against my sorrow in the night,
those crimson blossoms always bring me cheer.
He watches from above where all is bright.
Somehow they make it seem that he is near.

Those crimson blossoms always bring me cheer.
They light my way when darkness hides the sky.
Somehow they make it seem that he is near.
I cherish them until they fade and die.

They light my way when darkness hides the sky.
When autumn comes, I know they must depart.
I cherish them until they fade and die.
He sends a gift to soothe my aching heart.

When autumn comes, I know they must depart.
Although he closed his eyes and slipped away,
he sends a gift to soothe my aching heart.
He sends me roses for our special day.

IOWA POETRY ASSOCIATION AWARD, CONTEST 44 (POETRY FOR CHILDREN)
First Place, Martha H. Balph, Millville, UT

Spinach

Yucky green stuff on my plate—
I'm told to EAT the thing I hate.
If only it could magically
Get eaten up—but not by me.

Looking down from where I'm seated
Makes me think of what might eat it.
Carpet's green, and so is spinach:
Feed the rug what I can't finish!

Now my plate is clean and white—
All the spinach out of sight.
Do you think I'll get a pardon
If Mom finds my secret garden?

IOWA POETRY ASSOCIATION AWARD, CONTEST 44 (POETRY FOR CHILDREN)
Second Place, Linda R. Payne, Cincinnati, OH

Summer Rain

Who's that tapping on my window
with their pitter-patter fingers?
"Come outside and join our splashing,"
call the dancing raindrop singers.

Sail your leaf-boats in the gutters;
do a splashing puddle dance.
Hurry now the clouds get thinner
this may be our only chance, for

Soon the raindrop dance is over
as the sun peeks out his head.
With a curtsy, raindrops yield and
leave a rainbow in their stead.

IOWA POETRY ASSOCIATION AWARD, CONTEST 44 (POETRY FOR CHILDREN)
Third Place, Marjorie Dohlman, Riceville, IA

A to Zoo

Acrobatic armadillo
Balancing beaver
Cartwheeling caribou
Doodling donkey
Exercising elephant
Flipping fox
Gargling goat
Hiccuping hyena
Incognito ibex
Jiggling jaguar
Kissing koala
Leaning llama
Marching moose
Neon narwhal
Operatic ocelot
Prancing platypus
Quavering quail
Ricocheting rabbit
Slapping sloth
Tapdancing turtle
Undulating uakari
Vanishing vulture
Waltzing wallaby
Xylophoning xerus
Yammering yak
Zany zoo

WYOPOETS AWARD, Contest 45 (Wyoming or The West)

First Place, Susan Daubenspeck, Corpus Christi, TX

Singing Red Sky

Before dawn, out my kitchen window
Outline across the meadow
Where yesterday's grass was matted
By a few head of Black Angus cattle—
Who nibbled hidden stalks
As if they were thoughts
To be pulled up and chewed on overnight.

The outline is the trees' dark horizon
Far as a lazy eye can see
And this wanting in my bones
As I lean against the sink:
Not just for the singing of the red sky
But for the owls to arrive
And settle in to dream.

On my window sill reside two porcelain chickens
And one rooster.
They were once my mother's.
Now they are larks of my sodden nostalgia.

I've nailed two wooden pictures of
Owls on either side of them
As a talisman. As balance.

Faint light, a half kiss
Brushes onto Perry Road. Between meadow
And window, commuters stream in
Headlight dances.

Singing red sky.
I bite at corners of a piece of toast
Made from days old bread,
Start breakfast for the others
And bed down further in myself
An owl in her kitchen tree.

WYOPOETS AWARD, CONTEST 45 (WYOMING OR THE WEST)
Second Place, Cheryl A. Van Beek, Wesley Chapel, FL

Enchanted

Erupted from sea floor, earth turned inside out
sandstone fingers reach up—pray
to white-smoked lapis lazuli sky.
Energy masses in the hoodoos—
Cathedral Rock's magnetite pull,
quartz's electric pulse
through Bell Rock, their red stone blood.

Cactus needles shoot yellow-petaled stars.
Hummingbirds wear purple crowns,
whir, whiz through fiery air, slice
the smolder with tiny propellers.
Tangles of jasmine wrangle parched air,
pinwheel their white perfume.
Light glazes a glassy chapel
chiseled in cinnamon-colored cliffs,
glistens its hymn over the desert.

Here was a force that petrified
dinosaurs' conifer forest—felled and split logs
as if they were pistachio shells,
jeweled their veins with silica and minerals,
hoodooed the wood, turned it to stone—
where agate glass colors swirl,
mock the rock-bark that traps them.

Spirit sprinkled the potion of sand and silt
from a bygone sea, layer-painted
the desert scarlet, gold and aubergine.

Shell fossils remember an ocean that once owned
the chasm where the Colorado River carved
a canyon so grand its wonder
echoes through the Badland.

WYOPOETS AWARD, CONTEST 45 (WYOMING OR THE WEST)

Third Place, O. William Asplund, Layton, UT

Roundup Memories

Uncle Clifford was my Dad's best friend.
They married sisters.
Both were self-made men in the cattle business,
who loved to compete at everything,
so our herd was Herefords,
my uncle's herd was Angus,
white face or black.
Going to the Pincher Creek Station cattle sale was a delight,
great fun to watch them bid against each other.
In parades my dad rode his Kentucky Walking Horse stallion,
my uncle preferred his Palomino mare.
They were both ribbon rich.
Our ranch was the Flying Circle,
Uncle Clifford leased the Sundance Ranch
where the Piegan Blackfeet held their summer rituals.

But both men knew when it was time to cooperate,
everyone pitched in at the fall roundup.
My uncle did the branding,
while my dad castrated the bull calves.
Dad would spit on his whet stone
and sharpen the Sheffield steel blade of his pocket knife
by sliding it back and forth till it was razor sharp.
It was the same knife used to cut cheese and bologna rounds
when we stopped and ate lunch.
Both men worked fast which was lucky for me
since I grabbed and held on to the hind legs during the surgeries.
Hard, dirty, satisfying work.
Kicked, bruised and sore at the end of the day.
In the experiences of my youth this is near the top
and amazingly both men still had enough energy to argue
the merits of Herefords versus Angus on the way home.

The Grandfather Clock

The massive clock he carved from boards of oak,
is now a sentinel in my front hall.
It wears his essence like a wooden cloak,
and rouses me each hour with its call.
I watched him carve, emboss the leaves to life
the pinnate edges rose in perfect shape,
each vein and rib emerging as the knife
slipped in with force the grain could not escape.
But once the surface held against the blade
the point came up to nick the artist's thumb,
and spatter marked the wood a darker shade.
Now in the shadow of the pendulum

a blossom stain that no one else can see
reminds of blood that marked the oak and me.

Second Place, Lorraine Jeffery, Orem, UT

Canning

Harvest wall in pale pears, blushing
        peaches, tangy
        tomatoes crushed and jammed
        tight sweetness squeezed from royal grapes, orange
        magenta jams and jellies
        heavy on the shelf.

Mason bottles chronicle fruit flies and wasps,
        peeling, blanching,
        packing, steaming,
        pucker of plums on my tongue. The syncopated
        pop of sealing lids,

speak of huge metal bowls, salt,
        browning fruit, ripe
        pears' pregnant perfume, sticky
        floors and counters. Slippery
        fruit sliding down glass, remembers
        grandmotherly skills, rationed
        sugar, worm holes and rotting
        centers scooped out.

Phalanx of jars,
        packed and sealed against
        a leafless winter—
        no seal against
        loneliness.

SAN ANTONIO POETS ASSOCIATION AWARD, CONTEST 46 (HOMEMADE WITH LOVE)
Third Place, Robert Schinzel, Highland Village, TX

Kachinas on First Mesa

Talahytewa steps around cobbles
in Moenkopi Wash as he searches
for the right cottonwood,
one with roots that go deep,
tap the essence of the earth,
wood growing underground
far superior to trunks above.
When he finds a suitable tree,
he digs and cuts with care
to maintain harmony in the universe,
careful to avoid *koyaanisqátsi*,
life out of balance.
Kokopelli, Hopi's kachina deity of fertility,
whispers guidance to Talahytewa, a carver
who makes a doll in the spirit's likeness.
Talahytewa's oldest daughter
and her husband, married more than a year,
have no child. The kachina doll will help.

Dances begin on First Mesa.
A flute, Kokopelli's instrument of choice,
joins the winds from the north in song
as winter solstice approaches,
sending signals of change.
Spring will soon enough arrive
when maidens with round bellies
plant corn and squash.

MAINE POETS SOCIETY AWARD, CONTEST 47 (THE SEA OR SEACOAST)
First Place, Crystie Cook, Sandy, UT

Observation at Oceanside Beach, California

Here, pelicans rule the pier.
As seabirds go, they are homely, solid but lanky lieutenants
with the uncommon combination
of grisly, gray awkwardness and lustrous, white feathers.
They peer down their bills, unconcerned
by barnacles and masses of mussels
stuck to support beams below,
because after all, they, too,
must brave the leaping tide
as it rises in its cold, coughing wrath.
How proudly the birds perch,
clamped to the wooden rails
like large reading lamps all folded up,
with the splendid, shrunken drapery
of their great, jowled pouches,
to wait as patiently as the oldest fisherman here,
then occasionally shake their heads
at irreverent seagulls and cheeky children.
Their long-sleeved wings feel equally at home
kiting on the uppermost air current,
or swimming on the surface of the Pacific
and gliding like guitarfish,
or under the water
as they dive into the sea for small surfperch.
They shun long, slimy seaweed
with those globulous bulbs of gooey sea-pus,
and they are more than wise enough
to stare point-blank at human fishermen,
just to gauge the likelihood of retaliation
should the salty, top layer of a bucket of bait
go harmlessly missing.

MAINE POETS SOCIETY AWARD, CONTEST 47 (THE SEA OR SEACOAST)
Second Place, Christine H. Boldt, Temple, TX

The Compass Rose

Conscience is man's compass, and though the needle sometimes deviates, though one often perceives irregularities when directing one's course by it, one must still try to follow its direction. ~Vincent Van Gogh

Our mother lived her spiritual life full sail,
reaching from one golden shore to another.
She praised her Lord, at first, in Baptist pews
then knelt to sip the cup at a high church rail.
And next, she devoted herself to Mary.
Every time she tacked, we followed in her wake:

to the Sunday School where we crayoned crosses,
shouted praise, and sang of waters rolling down;
to the dim sanctuary where our fidgets
were subsumed in quiet, holy, staring
at the sad-eyed, stained-glass man
who stilled a window's storming sea;
to the marble vault where waters were confined
in stoup and font, and we peeked between our
folded fingers, at that fearsome, flaming heart.

But the higher the wind, the rougher the waves.
She nearly foundered on a chartless passage
in a following sea. That was when we all lost
our bearings for a while. At last, becalmed,
we put in at a storefront that smelled of coffee
and the need to wash, where the only chanteys sung
were of men and women, spirit and true north…
doing what one could. The best that *she* could do
was to tell us kids whatever seemed true at the time.

That was our only haven.

Third Place, Julie Shavin, Fountain, CO

Hope's Cloak

The fish are falling to the bottom of the sea.
~Andrew Bellon

The time has come, I say, it is time to go.
But you insist on turning back the clocks.

From the dark, two cigarettes appear
out of thin air, because all the air is thin here.
Thin apples, thin thoughts.
One fag is for lighting, one for
contemplating black lung.

The oceans are dying, someone said,
which I had heard before,
half a year, a whole,
cannot cast it to a feeling.
I remember by brother's fish
when we were young,
all eventually just below the aquarium rim,
little bloated rainbows.

The fish are falling to the bottom.
Let's drink, I say breezily.
But you insist I am too thin to hold water,
and I notice you've come from the sea
soaked in seaweed and psychosis,
with a fresh net of stars.

MIRIAM S. STRAUSS MEMORIAL AWARD, Contest 48 (City Life)

First Place, Laura Trigg, Little Rock, AR

This Is the City That Birthed Me

I have felt the pulse of cars
pounding in her arteries.

I was taught in her schools,
her theaters and auditoriums.

I have run in the palms of her parks
and have sat on her shoulders
to watch her night lights twinkle.

I have touched the shimmering
necklace of her river.

I have watched some of my
many siblings mar her skin
and seen her heal her wounds.

I have seen her hands shape
the tall buildings and smooth
the jagged edges of decay.

This is the city that birthed me.
And I thank her.

From Up Here

Imagine Mondrian's lively lines like a builder's
snapped chalk line across the city—clearly
this is not the rambling European city or
the western town that grew up along paths
of natives and animals. From a great height,
the artist's clean colors sing the bold and alert
city where we infer a populace of assorted cultures
and confessions and professions. Intersections
meet, well-bred and neat; squares punctuate the city
with fountains and benches for catching one's breath
mid-errand, warming winter-pinked face or cooling
unhatted heads in August breezes. Up here, we're
tempted to consider moving there and leave our
clouds to tend themselves. These could be cliffs
above traffic streams instead of banks and stores.
Apartment buildings shelter diurnal and nocturnal
life—diversely two foot, four foot, winged, horned
—and never monotony! Lights wink; horns and
whistles are aural flashes against footfalls and human
chatter. Who can hear whom? Over there a clutch
of church spires enlivens the cityscape
where a heroic mounted warrior guards
the town hall. Here are clever bus shelters,
avant-garde public art (by Mondrian's friends,
no doubt), and polished angles of steel and marble.
Shadows grow long on the street, crawl the curbs,
shrink to make room for moon shadows.
Men work here; women shop, and women work
here and men shop. Their lives give the city
breath, and every day they shape and reshape it
—not just an aping of art and more than art forming
the city. A child's graceless scribble, an anonymous
masterpiece—it's a home for many, a place to leave
for some, and it lives with that intentionality

MIRIAM S. STRAUSS MEMORIAL AWARD, Contest 48 (City Life)

of a human, which is to say, sane and crazy,
chaste and sexy, frugal and extravagant,
slapdash and meticulous—in short, the complete
thesaurus of words meaning life.

MIRIAM S. STRAUSS MEMORIAL AWARD, Contest 48 (City Life)

Third Place, Omair Hasan, Toledo, OH

Poetry open mic at a busy café but I do not speak

My mahogany corner table lies
between the bustling kitchen
and the cramped regulars reviewing
their iambic selections before gracing
the sandwich-and-decaf-sedated audience.
A rippling caramel cappuccino
tickles my tongue like traffic horns
blended into clear-sky creamer.

On these dimly-lit and muted evenings,
I am a hands-in-pockets
and whistle-while-you-work
type of background character
in every poet and café-goer's subplots.

I drain the coffee and listen
as it washes the city into my stomach—
intense dark chocolate *good mornings*
and hummingbird neon signs.

The brunette on stage stumbles over her
thigh-high boots and alliterated lyrics.
I disappear before she recovers
and stroll airily between quick-footed
pedestrians dusted with determination
and powdered sugar.

I hail a cab and I am one amongst one million
persons raising a hand sharply over the road.
Far too many taxis pass before one stops—
and all of a sudden—I am one in a million—
I place my hand on the roof and feel the taxi
muttering heartfelt *thank yous* from her exhaust
and glistening in her own moonlight.

THE POETS NORTHWEST AWARD, Contest 49 (Any Subject)

First Place, Gail Denham, Sunriver, OR

Evenings Among the Junipers

Junipers march up our hills, ignore
dust devils that whirl grit into their
gnarled limbs, like gangs of grade
school boys, daring anyone to stop them.

Winds cease their antics at dusk,
when bronze juniper trees become
silhouettes against the rising moon;
when jack rabbits begin to search
every shadow, crouch or leap
to avoid coyotes or owls.

Top of the hill, junipers seem to stand
aside, just a little, allowing a small
coyote pack to tune up for their evening
concert. Against bright moonlight, an elk
takes a majestic stroll, pauses now and then
to sniff the air and ripple his muscles.

If we could, we'd live here among this
wild world, sit on rough lava rocks, feel day
change to night, view brilliant star displays
here where no street lights interfere,
watch quail parades, follow lizard trails,
and learn to make juniper berry dyes.

The Challenge

It is not light that we need, but fire; it is not the gentle shower, but thunder. We need the storm, the whirlwind, and the earthquake.
~Frederick Douglas

It's not Plato's allegory, his gentle invitation
to abandon the cave's shadow and embrace the light,
or the plaintive call from Diogenes with his lantern,
as he looked for an honest man.
It's not Florence Nightingale, the lady with the lamp,
giving comfort to the wounded soldiers at night,
nor the Biblical "light of mine" that will bring today's change.

Instead,

It's the smelting furnace that turns iron-carbon into steel
to provide housing, factories and schools for the wretched,
and the blistering welds upon trolleys and trains
to transport those who stand ready for a job.
It's heat from the ovens that bring bread to the starved
and the zeal of debate, the passion of justice and right
that can show the blunder against one is a sin against all,
and an outcry for the common good
that will return the rivers' sparkle, the sky to azure blue.

THE POETS NORTHWEST AWARD, Contest 49 (Any Subject)
Third Place, Barbara Blanks, Garland, TX

Isolation
Echo Sonnet

Although she's by his side he walks alone.
She chatters endlessly—both with her thumbs
and with her voice, while he is left with crumbs
because she just can't disconnect her phone.

She's trapped within a solitary zone,
afraid of silence, dreads the emptiness
of life. She fills the void with screen's caress,
and simply cannot disconnect her phone.

He'd like to cast away addiction's stone
and free her from her cell—a prison break.
She doesn't seem to know his love's at stake,
because she just won't disconnect her phone.

Although she's by his side he walks alone,
because she just can't disconnect her phone.

aurelia

Troubled 29-Year-Old Helped to Die by Dutch Doctors
~BBC, August 2018

i hear voices all the time—   they say
you have hope   but there is no hope,
my words shriveling like skin   in my throat.

i'm not yet thirty.   they want to wait
a few more years   *it's not too late*
to change your mind   but my obituary is printed

on the insides of my eyelids   and unanswered prayers
have fled the mouth   like smoke
and small birds.   my mother says

i have a nice voice,   a voice made of light
but it doesn't match   my body, my face—
nothing matches. i light   a match. my hair won't catch

fire.   i cross days off with black ink
and a man in a suit   leads me inside
the crematorium   like a guest, but *please,*

don't stand for me.   i am no guest.
outside, sparrows shake—   snow settles
on the spokes   of chained bicycles.

aurelia: golden one, golden   apple of my mother's eye.
mother—   bedside, the doctor
downstairs, god   watching from the window.

i toast the barbiturate   to another life, touch
my wings   to the sparrows—
the sun is liquid gold   and i'm to become its messenger.

STUDENT AWARD, GRADES 9-12, CONTEST 50 (ANY SUBJECT)
Second Place, Krystal Smith, Little Rock, AR

Don't Shoot

Xavier Brown, a boy of color
who grew up around black men.
He watched his friends get murdered by cops
and thought his skin was a sin.
The slums of Chicago, that's where he lived.
Where bullets ran loose and free
and tears filled the homes of the families
that grieved, like fish fill up the sea.
Zay ran up on the white-lined field
and threw in his red mouthpiece.
For football was his only love,
an escape from the hateful police.
As he ran on the field he thought
about Shawn, the friend he lost at ten.
He had gone to the grocery store
one day, never to return again.
Zay fought back tears as he imagined Shawn
lying frightened and scared on the floor.
His eyes wide open, nearly glazed over,
shaken to the core.
Zay's tears turned to anger as he blocked
the middle man, thinking about Shawn's end.
Maybe cops like shooting bullets,
since killing blacks is a trend.
Zay wanted to scream as he ran down
the field, his hatred taking root.
Blood boiled within as he realized
his friend's last words were "please don't shoot."

STUDENT AWARD, GRADES 9-12, CONTEST 50 (ANY SUBJECT)

Third Place, Mary Margaret Sell, 9th Grade, Dallas, TX

Mackey Walks Me

A fat, wintry moon,
Drifts mindlessly in the heavens,
A golden dog,
Tail brandished in the soft hue of night.
A fierce force of instinct
Pulls his nose to the grass.
To smell the winter colors.
He looks behind,
Searching for the approval of his master.
Almond eyes trapped in the delicate state
Of fascination.
The dog leads the master,
To the patch of bare trees.
One lone survivor of the winter
Plays in the wind.
The dog leaps on his toned haunches,
Upwards to the sky, and the clouds.
Upwards.
A simple pup amidst the simple nature
Of the world outside the window.

INDEX BY AUTHOR

Altshul, Laura, "Family of Six Portrait, 1918" ... 95
Asplund, O. William, "Roundup Memories" ... 143
Bailey, Karen Kay, "The Neglected Gift" ... 81
Balph, Martha H., "Flight" ... 73
Balph, Martha H., "Spinach" ... 138
Barnes, Patricia, "Napping Baby" ... 43
Barney, V. Kimball, "Wishful Fishing" ... 107
Barton, Mark, "Sighting Birdsong in the Pyrenées" ... 82
Bell, Jean, "Shadow Crossing" ... 12
Bell, Jean, "Sarcasm in December" ... 75
Blanks, Barbara, "We're Not Going to Disneyland" ... 21
Blanks, Barbara, "Out for Blood" ... 59
Blanks, Barbara, "Yesterday" ... 83
Blanks, Barbara, "Like His Ancestors" ... 126
Blanks, Barbara, "Isolation" ... 156
Blenheim, Robert E., "A Wet Dream in a Dry Season" ... 51
Blenkush, Micki, "Riding the Down and Up Waves" ... 39
Blenkush, Micki, "This Year's Garden" ... 108
Blenkush, Micki, "From the Voice of Water" ... 131
Boldt, Christine H., "The Place for Lost Children" ... 86
Boldt, Christine H., "Middle School Choir Concert" ... 133
Boldt, Christine H., "The Compass Rose" ... 148
Bond, David, "Reanimation" ... 18
Bouma, Jana, "Postponement" ... 62
Breen, Nancy, "Virginia Specter" ... 46
Brown, Markay, "Undressing Billy Collins" ... 104
Campbell, Susan Maxwell, "Graft: Kisses and Roses" ... 115
Campbell, Susan Maxwell, "From Up Here" ... 151
Carlson, Maxine, "Note to His New Wife" ... 47
Chambers, Susan Stevens, "Planning a Poetry Party With a Cheese Head of Billy Collins" ... 4
Chisholm, Alison, "Double Exposure" ... 97
Chisholm, Alison, "One Moment In Time" ... 135
Conklin, Joshua, "Ode to the Cochlea" ... 102
Conklin, Joshua, "Questioning" ... 127
Cook, Crystie, "Against Time" ... 9
Cook, Crystie, "Booksmarts" ... 101
Cook, Crystie, "Observation at Oceanside Beach, California" ... 147
Cook, Meredith R., "Never Land Sixty-Six Years Later:" ... 53
Coppock, John, "Reflection " ... 44
Coppock, John, "from SYMPOSIUM—A Play: No. 1 and No. 2" ... 84

INDEX BY AUTHOR

Cotton, Kathy Lohrum, "A Few Slow Winter Bees" 22
Cotton, Kathy Lohrum, "Old Poet at the Open Mic" 29
Cotton, Kathy Lohrum, "Amargosa, the Hide-and-Seek River" 79
Cotton, Kathy Lohrum, "Two Views of the Plaza" 100
Cotton, Kathy Lohrum, "Lightning Rod" 103
Curry, Stephen, "Nature's Law" 78
Daubenspeck, Susan, "Singing Red Sky" 141
Denham, Gail, "Items I Read Last Year" 68
Denham, Gail, "Evenings Among The Junipers" 154
Diamond, Linda Eve, "Surreally Good Apple " 36
Dohlman, Marjorie, "A to Zoo" 140
Donovan, Charmaine Pappas, "Storm Phobia" 60
Feenstra, Judith, "Stray Cat Traveling" 116
Felt, Geraldine, "Saint Simons Island, Georgia" 26
Finnegan, Brenda Brown, "A Different Thanksgiving" 136
Flaugher, Christina M., "Letter to the Daughter I Didn't Have" 129
Funke, Barbara J., "The Invention of Nouns" 96
Fusco, Tony, "The Flag Is Upside Down" 66
Geil, Rita, "Directions for Daughters" 57
Glancy, Diane, "A Night on the Lake" 58
Glancy, Diane, "Yellowtail Lanes, Lodge Grass, Montana" 64
Glancy, Diane, "March" 77
Glancy, Diane, "Card Stock" 89
Gorrell, Dena R., "Sometimes All That Glitters Isn't Gold" 128
Gow, Robin, "flowers 1964" 38
Guinn, Fay, "Too Much Bliss" 88
Gunn, Gwen, "Earthmother" 17
Gunn, Gwen, "Found Gift" 42
Haltiner, Maurine, "Nosing About the Stars" 114
Hardesty, Jerri, "Wild Party" 33
Hardesty, Jerri, "Random Act" 106
Harvey, Dave, "Dale Bassett, 1922–77" 13
Harvey, Dave, "A Sign, a Jingle" 109
Harvey, Dave, "Deadly Birds" 112
Hasan, Omair, "Poetry open mic at a busy café but I do not speak" 153
Holcomb, J. Paul, "I Never Liked That Tie Anyway" 85
Holcomb, J. Paul, "Changing Seasons, Changing Colors" 125
Hurzeler, Richard, "Where Worlds Collide" 105
Irish, Amy, "The Winged Nike (of Nevada)" 36
Irish, Amy, "The Children of the Earth" 130

INDEX BY AUTHOR

Irving, Christine, "Rendezvous on Ithaca" 23
Jeffery, Lorraine, "Saved" 24
Jeffery, Lorraine, "New Bird Feeder" 119
Jeffery, Lorraine, "Canning" 145
Johnson, Caroline, "Cancer" 70
Johnson, Caroline, "On Listening to Middle Eastern Poetry at the Poetry Foundation in Chicago" 99
Jones, Doris, "Audience" 15
Jones, Doris, "Beachside Jazz" 41
Kolp, Laurie, "Community Comes Out in Troubled Times" 65
La Rocca, Lynda, "Autumn Ritual" 14
Lambert, Paula J, "Berkshire Mountains, September 2016" 11
Lambert, Paula J, "Siege" 67
Lee, Trina, "Somewhere" 121
Liu, Laura, "aurelia" 157
Mahan, Budd Powell, "When Spring Returns" 6
Mahan, Budd Powell, "The Vietnam Memorial" 111
Mahan, Budd Powell, "Smoke" 120
Mahan, Budd Powell, "Blood on the Mountain" 123
Mahan, Budd Powell, "The Grandfather Clock" 144
McBride, Andrea, "Writing Outside" 72
McCarthy, LaVern Spencer, "The Old, Yellow School Bus" 69
McCarthy, LaVern Spencer, "He Loves Me Still…" 137
Mele, James B., "August" 76
Miller, Terry, "A Whisper in Dime Box" 28
Montague, Kolette, "Flower Power" 22
Moore, Sheila, "Canary Island Caballero" 8
Moran, Catherine, "All the forgotten pieces" 71
Moran, Catherine, "Crisis hot-line" 87
Moran, Catherine, "Discovering pigs" 91
Morin, Sarah, "The Penguin" 16
Morin, Sarah, "Stalactite/Stalagmite" 80
Morin, Sarah, "Checklist For The Picnic" 118
Morris, Wilda, "On the Local Train from Orvieto to Florence, Italy" 1
Nankee, Cynthia, "(Not Quite) Still Life in the Garden: Black Cat with Pumpkins " 54
Payne, Linda R., "Summer Rain" 139
Pieczka, Patty Dickson, "Medieval Statue" 20
Salinas, Lisa Toth, "To the Former Child: Directions for Your Day" 113
Schinzel, Robert, "If Winter Comes…" 55
Schinzel, Robert, "Whiteout" 74
Schinzel, Robert, "A Long View Through Time" 110

INDEX BY AUTHOR

Schinzel, Robert, "Kachinas on First Mesa" 146
Schulte, Larry, "Home" 122
Sell, Mary Margaret, "Mackey Walks Me" 159
Shavin, Julie, "Judging the Cover" 52
Shavin, Julie, "Hope's Cloak" 149
Shiver, Joyce, "Cicada Summer" 124
Shute, Christian, "King of the Cul de Sac" 45
Smith, Krystal, "Don't Shoot" 158
Staas, Beth, "Family Album" 30
Staas, Beth, "Worship" 63
Staas, Beth, "Spring Demon" 132
Staas, Beth, "The Challenge" 155
Stone, Harvey, "The Drop" 32
Thrushart, Patricia, "The Churchgoer" 7
Tindall, Mary, "Doll" 90
Trigg, Laura, "This is the City That Birthed Me" 150
Tullis, Judith, "Georgia Bite" 25
Underwood, Pat, "Colostomy" 134
Van Beek, Cheryl A., "Enchanted" 142
Van Gerven, Claudia, "When the Trees Escaped" 48
Vevang, Curt, "The Grandpa Card" 117
Visser, Wendy, "Adrift" 61
Visser, Wendy, "Remnants" 93
Walker, Loretta Diane, "Aftermath" 98
Watson, Janet, "The Highest Range" 40
Watson, Janet, "At a Fundraiser for Cancer Victims" 92
Williams, Carol, "Long-Haired Cat" 56
Wilson, Lucille Morgan, "Tracks Through Winter" 94
Wolfe, Lorrie, "Marks on Paper" 49
Yanish, Marleine, "Becoming Music" 50

HONORABLE MENTIONS BY AUTHOR WITH CITY/STATE, CONTEST/AWARD

Ajami, Jocelyn, Chicago, IL, #6: 5th HM
Ajami, Jocelyn, Chicago, IL, #14: 5th HM
Alexander, Becky, Cambridge, Ontario, #34: 4th HM
Alligood, B. J., Port Orange, FL, #33: 3rd HM
Armstrong, Candace, Murphysboro, IL, #17: 5th HM
Austin-Hill, Suzanne E., Ruskin, FL, #10: 2nd HM
Baggett, Izzi, Dallas, TX, #50: 4th HM
Bailey, Karen Kay, Blanchard, OK, #30: 4th HM
Baldwin, Lisa E., Grants Pass, OR, #31: 3rd HM
Balph, Martha H., Millville, UT, #38: 1st HM
Balph, Martha H., Millville, UT, #5: 2nd HM
Balph, Martha H., Millville, UT, #17: 3rd HM
Balph, Martha H., Millville, UT, #43: 3rd HM
Balph, Martha H., Millville, UT, #4: 4th HM
Balph, Martha H., Millville, UT, #15: 4th HM
Balph, Martha H., Millville, UT, #12: 5th HM
Balph, Martha H., Millville, UT, #48: 5th HM
Balph, Martha H., Millville, UT, #49: 5th HM
Balph, Martha H., Millville, UT, #1: 6th HM
Balph, Martha H., Millville, UT, #25: 7th HM
Banks, Linda, Mesquite, TX, #45: 2nd HM
Banks, Linda, Mesquite, TX, #48: 3rd HM
Banks, Linda, Mesquite, TX, #49: 3rd HM
Banks, Linda, Mesquite, TX, #44: 4th HM
Barnes, Patricia, Wyandotte, MI, #28: 2nd HM
Barnes, Patricia, Wyandotte, MI, #34: 2nd HM
Barnes, Patricia, Wyandotte, MI, #30: 3rd HM
Barnes, Patricia, Wyandotte, MI, #7: 4th HM
Barnes, Patricia, Wyandotte, MI, #29: 4th HM
Barnes, Patricia, Wyandotte, MI, #39: 6th HM
Barnes, Patricia, Wyandotte, MI, #11: 7th HM
Barney, V. Kimball, Kaysville, UT, #9: 7th HM
Barton, Mark, Mechanicsburg, PA, #17: 7th HM
Bates, Milton J., Marquette, MI, #5: 5th HM
Bell, Jean, Evergreen, CO, #20: 2nd HM
Bell, Jean, Evergreen, CO, #40: 6th HM
Berry, Eleanor, Lyons, OR, #13: 2nd HM

Blanks, Barbara, Garland, TX, #47: 1st HM
Blanks, Barbara, Garland, TX, #11: 4th HM
Blanks, Barbara, Garland, TX, #21: 4th HM
Blanks, Barbara, Garland, TX, #31: 6th HM
Blanks, Barbara, Garland, TX, #13: 7th HM
Blenheim, Robert E., Daytona Beach, FL, #2: 5th HM
Blenheim, Robert E., Daytona Beach, FL, #39: 5th HM
Blenheim, Robert E., Daytona Beach, FL, #24: 7th HM
Blenheim, Robert E., Daytona Beach, FL, #47: 7th HM
Blenkush, Micki, St. Cloud, MN, #32: 2nd HM
Blenkush, Micki, St. Cloud, MN, #10: 6th HM
Boldt, Christine H., Temple, TX, #1: 2nd HM
Bond, David, Carbondale, IL, #3: 6th HM
Bourland, Von S., Happy, TX, #40: 3rd HM
Bourland, Von S., Happy, TX, #36: 7th HM
Breen, Nancy, Loveland, OH, #11: 2nd HM
Breen, Nancy, Loveland, OH, #29: 2nd HM
Brosnan, Jim, Assonet, MA, #8: 1st HM
Brown, Markay, St. George, UT, #21: 1st HM
Brown, Markay, St. George, UT, #46: 1st HM
Canerdy, Janice, Potts Camp, MS, #35: 5th HM
Carman, Jr., Howard S., Blountville, TN, #17: 2nd HM
Cates, Ann Carolyn, Southaven, MS, #21: 6th HM
Cates, Ann Carolyn, Southaven, MS, #33: 7th HM
Chambers, Susan Stevens, Good Thunder, MN, #5: 1st HM
Chambers, Susan Stevens, Good Thunder, MN, #1: 4th HM
Chambers, Susan Stevens, Good Thunder, MN, #10: 5th HM
Chambers, Susan Stevens, Good Thunder, MN, #15: 6th HM
Chisholm, Alison, Birkdale, U.K., #28: 3rd HM
Chisholm, Alison, Birkdale, U.K., #10: 4th HM
Chisholm, Alison, Birkdale, U.K., #39: 7th HM
Chisholm, Alison, Birkdale, U.K., #46: 7th HM
Christopherson, Nancy, Baker City, OR, #26: 4th HM
Christopherson, Nancy, Baker City, OR, #2: 6th HM
Clinesmith, Ryan, New York City, NY, #22: 5th HM
Conklin, Joshua, Amherst, NH, #47: 6th HM
Conte, Linda Haviland, Somerville, MA, #1: Citation

HONORABLE MENTIONS BY AUTHOR WITH CITY/STATE, CONTEST/AWARD

Cook, Crystie, Sandy, UT, #27: 3rd HM
Cook, Crystie, Sandy, UT, #6: 4th HM
Cook, Meredith R., Blue Earth, MN, #44: 2nd HM
Cook, Meredith R., Blue Earth, MN, #45: 3rd HM
Cook, Meredith R., Blue Earth, MN, #36: 4th HM
Cook, Meredith R., Blue Earth, MN, #33: 6th HM
Coppock, John, Tuttle, OK, #35: 1st HM
Coppock, John, Tuttle, OK, #30: 2nd HM
Coppock, John, Tuttle, OK, #19: 5th HM
Cotton, Kathy Lohrum, Anna, IL, #12: 1st HM
Cotton, Kathy Lohrum, Anna, IL, #42: 2nd HM
Cotton, Kathy Lohrum, Anna, IL, #26: 3rd HM
Cotton, Kathy Lohrum, Anna, IL, #21: 5th HM
Cotton, Kathy Lohrum, Anna, IL, #4: 6th HM
Cotton, Kathy Lohrum, Anna, IL, #16: 7th HM
Cotton, Kathy Lohrum, Anna, IL, #28: 7th HM
Couch, Mary A., Noblesville, IN, #34: 1st HM
Crawford, John W., Arkadelphia, AR, #45: 4th HM
Curry, Stephen, Jackson, MS, #12: 7th HM
Cuyler, Richard R., Middlebury, VT, #18: 1st HM
Daubenspeck, Susan, Corpus Christi, TX, #32: 1st HM
Daubenspeck, Susan, Corpus Christi, TX, #2: 3rd HM
Daubenspeck, Susan, Corpus Christi, TX, #8: 3rd HM
Davidson, Marc, Daytona Beach, FL, #24: 2nd HM
Davidson, Marc, Daytona Beach, FL, #13: 5th HM
Denham, Gail, Sunriver, OR, #45: 7th HM
Dial, Emma, Austin, TX, #50: 6th HM
Dohlman, Marjorie, Riceville, IA, #25: 2nd HM
Donovan, Charmaine Pappas, Brainerd, MN, #7: 1st HM
Donovan, Charmaine Pappas, Brainerd, MN, #22: 3rd HM
Donovan, Charmaine Pappas, Brainerd, MN, #42: 3rd HM
Donovan, Charmaine Pappas, Brainerd, MN, #31: 7th HM
Durmon, Pat, Norfork, AR, #17: 6th HM
Durmon, Pat, Norfork, AR, #41: 6th HM
Durmon, Pat, Norfork, AR, #22: 7th HM
Escoubas, Michael, Bloomington, IL, #2: 1st HM
Farmer, Lynn, Decatur, GA, #48: 2nd HM
Farmer, Lynn, Decatur, GA, #49: 2nd HM
Felt, Geraldine, Layton, UT, #38: 7th HM
Fiedler, Virginia Barrie, Evergreen, CO, #8: 6th HM
Flaugher, Christina, Mapleton, MN, #42: 5th HM
Floyd, Lin, St. George, UT, #29: 1st HM
Foster, John, Sun City Center, FL, #24: 1st HM
Foster, John, Sun City Center, FL, #42: 1st HM
Foster, John, Sun City Center, FL, #26: 7th HM
Funke, Barbara J., St. George, UT, #20: 6th HM
Fusco, Tony, West Haven, CT, #43: 6th HM
Geil, Rita, Carson City, NV, #9: 3rd HM
Geil, Rita, Carson City, NV, #14: 3rd HM
Geil, Rita, Carson City, NV, #29: 3rd HM
Geil, Rita, Carson City, NV, #47: 5th HM
Geller, Conrad, Ashburn, VA, #14: 6th HM
Gipson, Sara, Scott, AR, #19: 1st HM
Gipson, Sara, Scott, AR, #4: 2nd HM
Gipson, Sara, Scott, AR, #37: 2nd HM
Gipson, Sara, Scott, AR, #39: 2nd HM
Glancy, Diane, Gainesville, TX, #3: 2nd HM
Glancy, Diane, Gainesville, TX, #47: 2nd HM
Glancy, Diane, Gainesville, TX, #15: 3rd HM
Glancy, Diane, Gainesville, TX, #20: 4th HM
Glancy, Diane, Gainesville, TX, #34: 5th HM
Glancy, Diane, Gainesville, TX, #38: 6th HM
Glancy, Diane, Gainesville, TX, #43: 7th HM
Goetz, Lori Anne, Germantown, TN, #25: 3rd HM
Goetz, Lori Anne, Germantown, TN, #29: 7th HM
Gordon, Peter M., Orlando, FL, #34: 3rd HM
Gordon, Peter M., Orlando, FL, #30: 7th HM
Gorrell, Dena R., Edmond, OK, #35: 4th HM
Gorrell, Dena R., Edmond, OK, #36: 6th HM
Goschy, Deborah, Eagle Lake, MN, #13: 6th HM
Gunn, Gwen, Guilford, CT, #20: 7th HM
Guttigoli, Riya, Dallas, TX, #50: 1st HM
Haltiner, Maurine, Salt Lake City, UT, #12: 4th HM
Hamblen, K., Baton Rouge, LA, #32: 7th HM

HONORABLE MENTIONS BY AUTHOR WITH CITY/STATE, CONTEST/AWARD

Hardesty, Jerri, Brierfield, AL, #43: 4th HM
Harvey, Dave, Talent, OR, #27: 5th HM
Hasan, Omair, Toledo, OH, #19: 3rd HM
Hill, Judyth, Conifer, CO, #1: 5th HM
Holcomb, J. Paul, Double Oak, TX, #18: 2nd HM
Holcomb, J. Paul, Double Oak, TX, #31: 4th HM
Holcomb, J. Paul, Double Oak, TX, #41: 5th HM
Holcomb, J. Paul, Double Oak, TX, #14: 7th HM
Horrocks, Elizabeth, Wilmslow, U.K., #9: 1st HM
Horrocks, Elizabeth, Wilmslow, U.K., #16: 2nd HM
Horrocks, Elizabeth, Wilmslow, U.K., #35: 2nd HM
Hudson, Mark, Evanston, IL, #27: 1st HM
Hughes, Mary Willette, Waite Park, MN, #9: 4th HM
Irish, Amy, Lakewood, CO, #22: 2nd HM
Irving, Christine, Denton, TX, #12: 3rd HM
Irving, Christine, Denton, TX, #1: Citation
Jeffery, Lorraine, Orem, UT, #27: 2nd HM
Jeffery, Lorraine, Orem, UT, #3: 7th HM
Jeffery, Lorraine, Orem, UT, #23: 7th HM
Jepson-Gilbert, Anita, Westminster, CO, #36: 5th HM
Johnson, Caroline, Willow Springs, IL, #6: 2nd HM
Johnson, Caroline, Willow Springs, IL, #12: 2nd HM
Johnson, Caroline, Willow Springs, IL, #16: 6th HM
Jones, Doris, Madison, MS, #25: 1st HM
Jones, Doris, Madison, MS, #15: 2nd HM
Jones, Doris, Madison, MS, #2: 4th HM
Jones, Doris, Madison, MS, #7: 5th HM
Jones, Doris, Madison, MS, #29: Citation
Jones, Emory D., Iuka, MS, #24: 3rd HM
Jones, Emory D., Iuka, MS, #45: 6th HM
Jones, Libby, Berea, KY, #14: 4th HM
Jones, Libby, Berea, KY, #28: 6th HM
Jones, Marcia, Golden, CO, #4: 5th HM
Jones, Marcia, Golden, CO, #8: 7th HM
Joyce, Beverly A., Land O'Lakes, FL, #37: 4th HM
Kincanon, Lynn, Loveland, CO, #27: 4th HM
Klinger, Gloria, Grand Haven, MI, #20: 3rd HM
Klinger, Gloria, Grand Haven, MI, #31: 5th HM
Klix, Rose, Johnson City, TN, #2: 2nd HM
Koch, Patricia Jo, Oklahoma City, OK, #18: 5th HM
Kohanski, Maxine, Spring, TX, #2: 7th HM
Kolp, Laurie, Beaumont, TX, #44: 5th HM
Krotz, Anita M., Salt Lake City, UT, #11: 5th HM
Krotz, Anita M., Salt Lake City, UT, #31: Citation
Kyler, Inge Logenburg, Eaton Rapids, MI, #39: 1st HM
Kyler, Inge Logenburg, Eaton Rapids, MI, #35: 3rd HM
L'Herisson, Catherine, Garland, TX, #36: 1st HM
L'Herisson, Catherine, Garland, TX, #33: 4th HM
La Fleur, Robert, Ponsford, MN, #26: 1st HM
La Fleur, Robert, Ponsford, MN, #23: 2nd HM
La Fleur, Robert, Ponsford, MN, #5: 3rd HM
La Fleur, Robert, Ponsford, MN, #22: 6th HM
La Rocca, Lynda, Salida, CO, #18: 3rd HM
La Rocca, Lynda, Salida, CO, #40: 4th HM
La Rocca, Lynda, Salida, CO, #33: 5th HM
La Rocca, Lynda, Salida, CO, #29: 6th HM
Lacy, Kate, Fayetteville, AR, #1: Citation
Lager, Ellen, Robbinsdale, MN, #15: 5th HM
Lambert, Paula J., Dublin, OH, #41: 1st HM
Lambert, Paula J., Dublin, OH, #38: 2nd HM
Lee, Trina, Oklahoma City, OK, #40: 7th HM
Leitch, Steven, West Jordan, UT, #17: 1st HM
Leitch, Steven, West Jordan, UT, #8: 2nd HM
Leitch, Steven, West Jordan, UT, #3: 4th HM
Mahan, Budd Powell, Dallas, TX, #6: 1st HM
Mahan, Budd Powell, Dallas, TX, #15: 1st HM
Mahan, Budd Powell, Dallas, TX, #40: 2nd HM
Mahan, Budd Powell, Dallas, TX, #16: 5th HM
Mahan, Budd Powell, Dallas, TX, #37: 6th HM
McBride, John, Bettendorf, IA, #31: 2nd HM
McBride, Andrea, Wesley Chapel, FL, #6: 3rd HM
McBride, John, Bettendorf, IA, #34: 7th HM
McCarthy, LaVern Spencer, Blair, OK, #9: 2nd HM
McCarthy, LaVern Spencer, Blair, OK, #26: 2nd HM

McCarthy, LaVern Spencer, Blair, OK, #1: 3rd HM
McCarthy, LaVern Spencer, Blair, OK, #46: 3rd HM
McCarthy, LaVern Spencer, Blair, OK, #8: 4th HM
McCarthy, LaVern Spencer, Blair, OK, #37: 5th HM
McCarthy, LaVern Spencer, Blair, OK, #30: 6th HM
McCarthy, LaVern Spencer, Blair, OK, #35: 6th HM
McDowell, Joy, Springfield, OR, #42: 6th HM
McVey, Jackie, Tyler, TX, #3: 5th HM
Miele, Cristiana, Forney, TX, #50: 7th HM
Miele, Gina, Forney, TX, #50: 3rd HM
Miller, Kari D., Evergreen, CO, #41: 7th HM
Miller, Terry, Richmond, TX, #16: 1st HM
Miller, Terry, Richmond, TX, #21: 3rd HM
Montague, Kolette, Centerville, UT, #19: 6th HM
Montague, Kolette, Centerville, UT, #46: 6th HM
Montague, Kolette, Centerville, UT, #15: 7th HM
Montague, Kolette, Centerville, UT, #27: 7th HM
Moore, Sheila, San Antonio, TX, #26: 6th HM
Moore, Sheila, San Antonio, TX, #21: 7th HM
Moran, Catherine, Little Rock, AR, #30: 1st HM
Moran, Catherine, Little Rock, AR, #9: 6th HM
Morin, Sarah, Fishers, IN, #19: 2nd HM
Morin, Sarah, Fishers, IN, #23: 4th HM
Morin, Sarah, Fishers, IN, #46: 5th HM
Moritz, Rita Aiken, Pell City, AL, #18: 7th HM
Morley, Diana, Talent, OR, #27: 6th HM
Morris, Karen McAferty, Pensacola, FL, #28: 5th HM
Morris, Wilda, Bolingbrook, IL, #48: 1st HM
Morris, Wilda, Bolingbrook, IL, #49: 1st HM
Morris, Wilda, Bolingbrook, IL, #16: 3rd HM
Morris, Wilda, Bolingbrook, IL, #26: 5th HM
Mortenson, Virginia, Des Moines, IA, #3: 1st HM
Mortenson, Virginia, Des Moines, IA, #11: 3rd HM
Mortenson, Virginia, Des Moines, IA, #38: 3rd HM
Nankee, Cynthia, Canton, MI, #44: 1st HM
Nankee, Cynthia, Canton, MI, #13: 4th HM
Nankee, Cynthia, Canton, MI, #41: 4th HM
Neff, Diane, Longwood, FL, #28: 4th HM
Opsahl, Polly, Oscoda, MI, #36: 3rd HM
Palfrey, Diane Attwell, Cambridge, Ontario, #32: 6th HM
Pamplin, P. Adrianne, Longview, TX, #28: 1st HM
Parr, Teresa, St. George, UT, #44: 3rd HM
Parr, Teresa, St. George, UT, #5: 4th HM
Parr, Teresa, St. George, UT, #30: 5th HM
Payne, Linda R., Cincinnati, OH, #43: 1st HM
Perreault, Chanel, Bedford, TX, #50: 5th HM
Peterson, Patricia A., Cottonwood Hts, UT, #7: 3rd HM
Picklesimer, Jeani M., Ashland, KY, #37: 7th HM
Pieczka, Patty Dickson, Carbondale, IL, #17: 4th HM
Pierce, Regan, Dallas, TX, #50: 2nd HM
Powers, Edith, Albuquerque, NM, #24: 5th HM
Pucciani, Donna, Wheaton, IL, #32: 4th HM
Pucciani, Donna, Wheaton, IL, #6: 7th HM
Reeder, Ray, Albuquerque, NM, #23: 3rd HM
Reeder, Ray, Albuquerque, NM, #25: 5th HM
Robinson, Kathleen, Champaign, IL, #25: 4th HM
Robinson, Kathleen, Champaign, IL, #47: 4th HM
Rood, Jennifer, Grants Pass, OR, #3: 3rd HM
Rood, Jennifer, Grants Pass, OR, #9: 5th HM
Rowley, Jo-Anne, Lafayette, CO, #32: 5th HM
Ruth, Janet, Corrales, NM, #4: 1st HM
Ruth, Janet, Corrales, NM, #45: 1st HM
Saidi, Mo, San Antonio, TX, #24: 6th HM
Saidi, Mo, San Antonio, TX, #13: Citation
Salinas, Lisa Toth, Spring, TX, #47: 3rd HM
Salinas, Lisa Toth, Spring, TX, #22: 4th HM
Salinas, Lisa Toth, Spring, TX, #46: 4th HM
Schinzel, Robert, Highland Village, TX, #7: 2nd HM
Schinzel, Robert, Highland Village, TX, #33: 2nd HM
Schinzel, Robert, Highland Village, TX, #42: 4th HM
Schinzel, Robert, Highland Village, TX, #25: 6th HM
Schinzel, Robert, Highland Village, TX, #19: 7th HM
Schwartz, Randy K., Ann Arbor, MI, #20: 5th HM
Schwartz, Randy K., Ann Arbor, MI, #48: 6th HM

HONORABLE MENTIONS BY AUTHOR WITH CITY/STATE, CONTEST/AWARD

Schwartz, Randy K., Ann Arbor, MI, #49: 6th HM
Sebba, Jon, Murray, UT, #24: 4th HM
Shea, Pegi Dietz, Rockville, CT, #11: 1st HM
Shea, Pegi Dietz, Rockville, CT, #44: 6th HM
Shepherd, Barbara, Edmond, OK, #40: 5th HM
Shepherd, Barbara, Edmond, OK, #44: 7th HM
Shiver, Joyce, Crystal River, FL, #34: 6th HM
Shiver, Joyce, Crystal River, FL, #35: 7th HM
Shiver, Joyce, Crystal River, FL, #48: 7th HM
Shiver, Joyce, Crystal River, FL, #49: 7th HM
Span, Amanda Grace, Sewickley, PA, #38: 5th HM
Staas, Beth, Oak Brook, IL, #31: 1st HM
Stanko, Mary Rudbeck, London, ON, #20: 1st HM
Stone, Harvey, Johnson City, TN, #48: 4th HM
Stone, Harvey, Johnson City, TN, #49: 4th HM
Strauss, Russell H., Memphis, TN, #13: 3rd HM
Strauss, Russell H., Memphis, TN, #37: 3rd HM
Strauss, Russell H., Memphis, TN, #16: 4th HM
Strauss, Russell H., Memphis, TN, #39: 4th HM
Strauss, Russell H., Memphis, TN, #43: 5th HM
Strauss, Russell H., Memphis, TN, #18: 6th HM
Sutton, Sheri A., Wichita Falls, TX, #39: 3rd HM
Tennant, Colette, Salem, OR, #10: 1st HM
Thompson, Carol, Tyler, TX, #7: 6th HM
Tullis, Judith, Indian Head Park, IL, #41: 2nd HM
Ulisse, Peter, Stratford, CT, #42: 7th HM
Underwood, Pat, Colfax, IA, #4: 7th HM
Van Beek, Cheryl A., Wesley Chapel, FL, #41: 3rd HM
Van Beek, Cheryl A., Wesley Chapel, FL, #29: 5th HM
Van Beek, Cheryl A., Wesley Chapel, FL, #11: 6th HM
Van Lenning, Ryan, Oakland, CA, #14: 1st HM
Verven, Eleni, Houston, TX, #1: Citation, 3rd grader
Visser, Wendy, Cambridge, Ontario, #10: 3rd HM
Volk, Benita, Denver, CO, #8: 5th HM
Wahl, Mike, Athens, AL, #12: 6th HM
Wainwright, Lucia, Westcliffe, CO, #22: 1st HM
Wainwright, Lucia, Westcliffe, CO, #23: 1st HM
Wainwright, Lucia, Westcliffe, CO, #32: 3rd HM
Wainwright, Lucia, Westcliffe, CO, #1: 7th HM
Walker, Loretta Diane, Odessa, TX, #13: 1st HM
Walters, S. Evan, Lebanon, IN, #46: 2nd HM
Walton, Caroline, Crystal River, FL, #33: 1st HM
Walton, Caroline, Crystal River, FL, #37: 1st HM
Walton, Caroline, Crystal River, FL, #40: 1st HM
Walton, Caroline, Crystal River, FL, #18: 4th HM
Watson, Janet, Wesley Chapel, FL, #43: 2nd HM
Watson, Janet, Wesley Chapel, FL, #19: 4th HM
Watson, Janet, Wesley Chapel, FL, #23: 6th HM
Watson, Janet, Wesley Chapel, FL, #7: 7th HM
Watson, Janet, Wesley Chapel, FL, #10: 7th HM
Whitney, Tanya R., Sorrento, LA, #45: 5th HM
Williams, Carol, York, PA, #14: 2nd HM
Williams, Carol, York, PA, #5: 6th HM
Wilson, Lucille Morgan, Des Moines, IA, #36: 2nd HM
Wolfe, Lorrie, Windsor, CO, #6: 6th HM
Young, S. A. (Sidney A.), Santa Fe, NM, #4: 3rd HM
Zimmerman, Elaine, Hamden, CT, #21: 2nd HM
Zimmerman, Elaine, Hamden, CT, #38: 4th HM
Zimmerman, Elaine, Hamden, CT, #23: 5th HM
Zimmerman, Elaine, Hamden, CT, #5: 7th HM

2019 CONTESTS

1. NFSPS Founders Award
2. The Diamond T Award
3. The NFSPS Board Award
4. The Margo Award
5. Winners' Circle Award
6. Donald Stodghill Memorial Award
7. Georgia Poetry Society Award
8. Poetry Society of Texas Award
9. The Children's Hour Award
10. Al Laster Memorial Award
11. Florida State Poets Association, Inc. Award
12. Alabama State Poetry Society Award
13. Land of Enchantment Award
14. The Virginia Corrie-Cozart Memorial Award
15. Arizona State Poetry Society Award
16. Mildred Vorpahl Baass Remembrance Award
17. League of Minnesota Poets Award
18. Jessica C. Saunders Memorial Award
19. Poetry Society of Indiana Award
20. Nevada Poetry Society Award
21. William Stafford Memorial Award
22. The New York Poetry Forum Award
23. Columbine Poets of Colorado Award
24. Morton D. Prouty & Elsie S. Prouty Memorial
25. Poets' Roundtable of Arkansas Award
26. Louisiana State Poetry Society Award
27. Freeda Murphy Memorial Award
28. Claire Van Breeman Downes Memorial Award
29. Utah State Poetry Society Award
30. CSPS James E. MacWhinney Memorial Award
31. Illinois State Poetry Society Award
32. Ohio Award
33. Minute Award
34. Poetry Society of Michigan Award
35. Mississippi Poetry Society Award
36. Jesse Stuart Memorial Award
37. Humorous Poetry Award
38. Barbara Stevens Memorial Award
39. Alice Mackenzie Swaim Memorial Award
40. Poetry Society of Oklahoma Award
41. Save Our Earth Award
42. Massachusetts State Poetry Society Award
43. Poetry Society of Tennessee Award
44. Iowa Poetry Association Award
45. Wyopoets Award
46. San Antonio Poets Association Award
47. Maine Poets Society Award
48. Miriam S. Strauss Memorial Award
49. The Poets Northwest Award
50. Student (Grades 9-12) Award

Made in the USA
Columbia, SC
19 June 2021